The Naval Battle of Mobile Bay
August 5, 1864
&
Franklin Buchanan on the *Tennessee*
A Portrait of the Admiral of the Confederate Fleet in Mobile Bay

by Francis X. Walter
Copyright 2010
Third Edition, Revised

ISBN: 0-9639140-1-4

Published by
USS Alabama Battleship Commission
P.O. Box 65
Mobile, Alabama 36601
www.ussalabama.com

Dedicated to the Memory
of
Hatchett Chandler
1881-1967

This romantic original and courtly old charmer, who turned his low-pay job as state groundskeeper at Fort Morgan into that of self-appointed promoter and historiographer; who lived lonely in a cavalry stable and nightly played his piano to the roar of the Gulf on his right and the sough of the Bay on his left; who did, said, wrote anything—true or not so true, wise or foolish—to preserve his beloved fort and its sandy point; who long ago let some boys from Mobile camp in its bastions, tunnel its buried arches, dig its shot and shell, learn its story and enjoy its oleanders, to him be thanks.

Acknowledgments
To Faye Walter, supporting wife
To Robin McLendon, creative graphic designer
To Pat Cather, encouraging bibliophile

Contents

Illustrations   2
Introduction   3

The Naval Battle of Mobile Bay

I. Mobile as a Military Objective   6
II. The Odds   14
III. A Battle in Four Acts   24
    Act One: Balanced to Partners   24
    Act Two: The Narrow Channel   30
    Act Three: Four against Seventeen   39
    Act Four: The *Tennessee* Alone   43

Appendix   55
Bibliography   57

Franklin Buchanan on the *Tennessee*   58

Illustrations

Mobile and its Defenses	7
Artist on Board the *Brooklyn*	9
Mobile Bay	11
Admiral David Farragut	13
Mobile and its Defenses: A Federal Map	15
Fort Morgan and the Rebel Fleet	17
The *Tennessee*, side view	20
The *Tennessee*, top view	21
Admiral Franklin Buchanan	23
Plan of the Battle of August 5, 1864	27
Farragut's Fleet	32
Destruction of the Monitor *Tecumseh*	35
"After You, Sir."	36
The *Richmond* engaging the *Tennessee*	41
The *Hartford* engaging the *Tennessee*	47
Farragut's Victory in Mobile Bay	49
The *Tennessee* after the battle	53
Odysseus and the Sirens	54
Admiral Franklin Buchanan	59

INTRODUCTION

About a year ago I was thumbing through a 1952 issue of the now regrettably defunct *Alabama Historical Quarterly* and a brief but succinct article on the Battle of Mobile Bay caught my eye. I noticed that it was written by Francis Walter who I had come to know as a customer in my antiquarian book store in Birmingham.

The Naval Battle of Mobile Bay was actually written by Francis in 1951 when he was a student at Spring Hill College.

Though written with the encouragement of the late and beloved (by some) Hatchett Chandler—who was not always known for the accuracy of his historiography—the article was quite scholarly, making good use of contemporary and primary sources, as well as respected secondary accounts. Further, the article was well written; but then, one would expect no less from a member of Mobile's highly literate Walter family.

Though a journal article, the piece was published complete with separate title page (as was often the case with the *Alabama Historical Quarterly*'s more important contributions) so, because of a longtime interest in all aspects of Mobile's history, I carefully removed the article with its title page and had it bound in cloth.

With bound volume and pen for autographing in hand, I was ready for Francis when he next visited my store! He seemed pleasantly surprised that someone would call attention to and ask him to inscribe this study some forty years after it was written. To me, it was the opportunity to add yet another view to my collection of histories of the state's most famous Civil War battle and its related engagements and aftermath.

To be sure, there was already a wealth of material. Prominent among the published histories are the near contemporary accounts of C. C. Andrews and Foxhall Parker, both of whom were participants on the Federal side. Parker's book covers naval matters almost exclusively and the value of his account is enhanced by the inclusion of two large folding maps. Andrews' account, on the other hand, is a more broadly based narrative with extensive coverage of related land engagements, as well as the maritime action.

Scharf's *History of the Confederate States Navy* gives a good account from the Confederate viewpoint, though it must be considered secondary research. An excellent primary source from the same viewpoint can be found in editor Carter Smith, Jr.'s *Two Naval Journals: 1864.*

Another important but very rarely seen source covering life in Mobile under wartime conditions is *Incidents of Life in a Southern City During the War,* by William Rix. Many late nineteenth and early twentieth century soldiers' and officers' memoirs contain accounts of the various land and water engagements at Mobile. Naturally, these accounts vary greatly in veracity and interest. To pursue them, the reader will want to make use of the well-indexed *Civil War Books: A Critical Bibliography* compiled by historian Allan Nevins and others. Dabney Maury's *Recollections of a Virginian* may be the best such book, but there are others that are well worth the time it takes to search them out.

Robert Bell's useful but modestly annotated *Bibliography of Mobile* is also of some help in doing further reading. Of greater utility, however, is Sidney Smith's *Mobile: 1861-1865 Notes and a Bibliography.*

Finally, the serious researcher should not neglect two excellent and massive sources: *Official Records of the Union and Confederate Navies in the War of the Rebellion* and the collected issues of *The Confederate Veteran* magazine. Both of these serials have been reprinted recently, the latter with a massive, newly compiled index.

Of the later, secondary histories, Sister Elizabeth Goodrow's *Mobile During the Civil War* is notable for its scarcity if for nothing else (only 100 copies were printed according to a contemporary diary entry by prominent Mobile bookseller Cameron Plummer). Caldwell Delaney's *Confederate Mobile* is remarkable and unsurpassed as a pictorial depiction of the war's effect on the city. Peter Hamilton's *A Little Boy in Confederate Mobile* consists of recollections of the city's most important historian but this title fades into near insignificance when compared to the towering second edition of his history of Mobile's colonial period. Virgil Carrington Jones, a former North Alabama newspaperman, devotes much "quality time" to Mobile and its environs in his monumental three-volume set, *The Civil War at Sea*.

The list of accounts does not stop here. I own a thick 1,000-page manuscript history of the battle by former Mobile physician Wallace Marshall. Another Mobilian is currently working on what has been termed the "definitive" history. I hope to see *it* published someday.

There is always room for another Mobile title on my bookshelves, and that is why I encouraged Francis to republish his research paper as a book.

Here, then—in much revised and expanded form—is the fruition of that encouragement. As I sit here on my second-floor balcony overlooking the expanse of the Gulf just outside Mobile Bay and, more particularly, the ship channel where the action actually began, I read Francis' proofs with my heart, as well as my eyes, knowing how the battle ended. Yet, reading with my heart, especially in the eerie and atavistic quiet of Dauphin Island, I can just barely hear the explosions of the torpedoes that likely were never "damned" by Admiral Farragut and I can both feel and taste faintly the courage and audacity of the outgunned and outmanned Admiral Buchanan and his men. And I can empathize with the tragedy of those sailors on the *Tecumseh* whose lives were lost almost before the battle began. Our history is with us always.

Patrick Cather
Sand Castle
Dauphin Island
August 12, 1991

I
Mobile as a Military Objective

The position of Mobile and her defenses toward the close of the War Between the States made her reduction necessary to the North. Second to New Orleans, she was the largest and most prosperous city on the Gulf Coast, and New Orleans was captive. Mobile stood alone, the largest open seaport on the Gulf Coast.

It was true that she was tightly blockaded by the Federal fleet, but there were still blockade runners that would slip into the Bay, much to the embarrassment of the large and powerful blockade fleet.

The runners were few and far between, however, and it was actually Northern public opinion and not the fact itself that hastened the battle. Mobile newspapers gave the United States Navy department many a headache when they would jubilantly announce to all the arrival of another blockade runner in the city. They patriotically neglected to mention the size of most of the ships (under 50 tons); by the time the Northern newspapers hit upon the story, they would rise in righteous indignation severely censuring the naval department for its gross neglect and inefficiency.[1]

A more urgent reason for the battle (also promoted by patriotic newspapermen) was the reputed ironclad fleet building at Selma, a town above Mobile and connected by river to the Bay.[2] The Yankees realized that Mobile was a potential ironclad base, and the Southern Confederacy was also aware of this. However, because of lack of finances and lack of material, the few ships

---

[1] Richard S. West, *Gideon Welles, Lincoln's Navy department* (Indianapolis: Bobbs-Merrill Co., 1943), p. 276.
[2] West, p. 271.

Mobile and its Defenses

Harper's Weekly, May 31, 1862

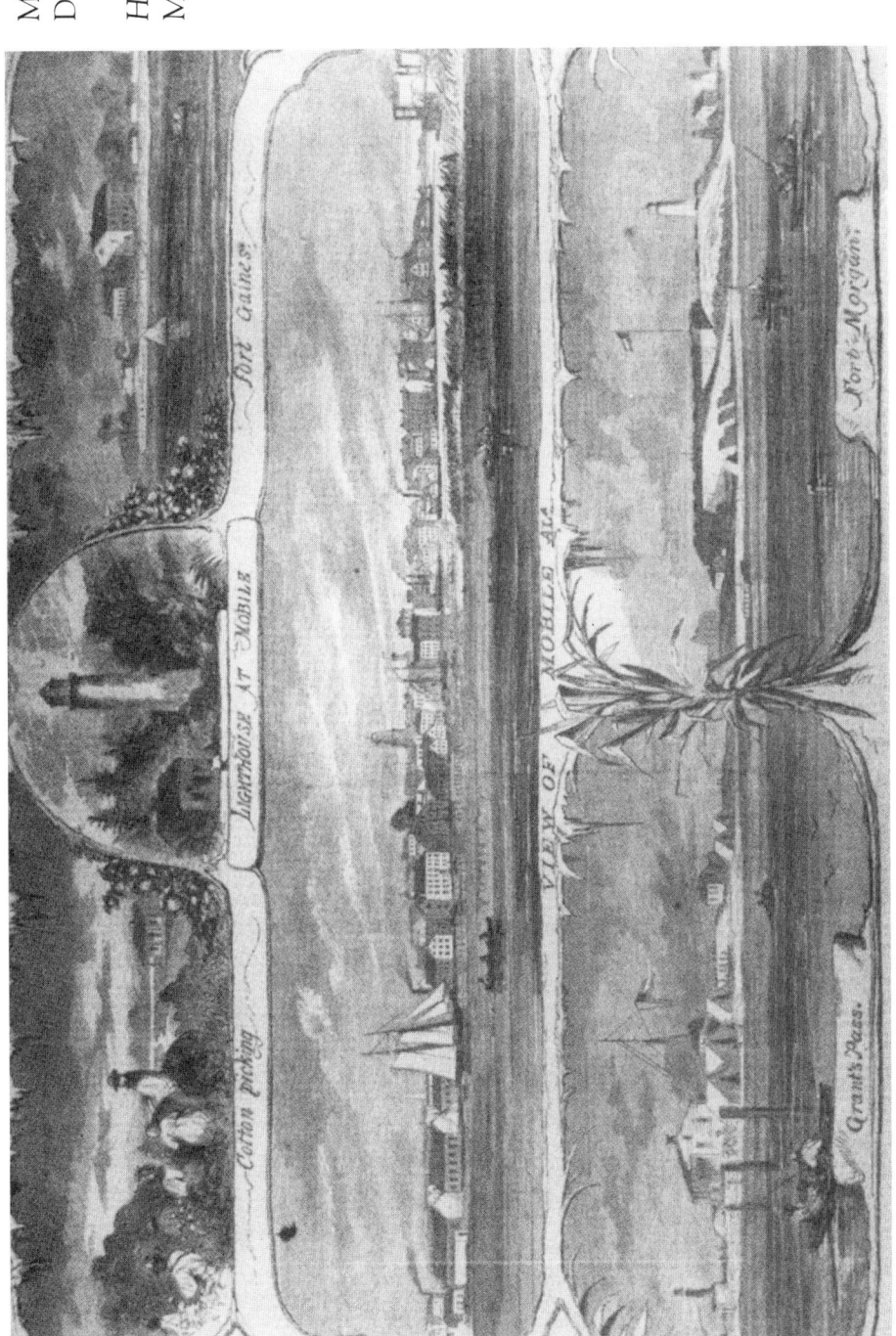

begun lay half-finished on the ways at Selma, never to be completed.

The newspapers, though, did their best to cover up the deficiencies, and when the Confederacy did get one ironclad built, the *Tennessee*, to serve in Mobile Bay, it was, thanks to the press, the most feared engine of war afloat.[3] It was said, up North, that if she ever got out of Mobile Bay, every port in the North would be at her mercy. Armchair admirals entreated the navy department to send every possible ironclad not absolutely needed elsewhere straight to Mobile Bay.

> ... and Secretary Welles of the Navy Department was scorched and slashed with criticism because of his seeming indifference to the portentous possibilities to the North threatened by this solitary Confederate ship.[4]

Thus it was that the destruction of the "solitary Confederate ship" was another reason for the reduction of Mobile.

A more serious reason was perhaps less known to the Northern public but well understood by the leaders of that day and

---

[3] "We are informed from pretty good authority that Admiral Buchanan, who has just returned from a trip of observation down the bay, determined upon an order which will materially add to the strength of the fleet which has been built and equipped to aid in the defence of Mobile. A crack raft, with a powerful battery and picked crew, ably and gallantly commanded in the *addendum*. This is the *avant courier* of the four other floating engines of war which will soon take their stations in the bay, and oppose their iron sides to the iron shot of the Federal Navy. The Federals will find out, after a while, 'that some things can be done as well as others,' and that Southern men may develop a genius for naval construction and warfare, as they have a splendid aptitude for fighting on *terra-firma*. Whether we gain these additions to our navy through cracks in the enemy's blockade, or by other means, we leave to him to find out or infer."— Mobile *Advertiser*, December 27, 1862.

[4] West, p. 271.

The apartment on the berth deck of the Brooklyn assigned to the staff artist of Harper's Weekly – as depicted by him.

Harper's Weekly, May 18, 1861

certainly well worried about. Northern strategists knew that if the *Tennessee* or any other force ever broke the Gulf blockade and opened a few cities to trade and commerce, England and France, who favored the South anyway, might enter the fight on the side of the South and destroy the whole blockade and the North, too, for the sake of commerce.[5] Fearing as they did the grossly exaggerated prowess of the *Tennessee,* they thought it possible that she could do this thing. They were therefore anxious to defeat Mobile and especially the *Tennessee,* the accomplishment of which would greatly boost the morale of the North and perhaps shock the tottering South into submission.

For the undertaking of this gigantic task, public opinion and Washington authorities selected Admiral David Glasgow Farragut. Farragut had deep roots in the South. Though born in Knoxville, Tennessee, in 1801, he was early familiar with the coast, especially New Orleans and the Mississippi Gulf coast. David Farragut's father, George Farragut (1755-1817), was a seafaring man and a key player in naval operations during the Revolutionary War. He owned a large plantation in Moss Point, Mississippi, and descendants in that region report that, during the war, Farragut often came ashore to visit his sister who lived in Pascagoula. There are many Farragut family members living on the Mississippi coast today.[6]

At the outbreak of hostilities, David Farragut faced the same moral choice faced by his future opponent in Mobile Bay, Franklin Buchanan: In the present dilemma, where does loyalty lie? Farragut was opposed to armed resistance against the Union and remained with the Federal navy. Buchanan resigned his commission and threw in with the Confederacy.

---

[5] J. T. Scharf, *History of the Confederate States Navy* (New York: Rogers and Sherwood, 1887).
[6] *Mobile Press Register,* Sunday, August 5, 1979, "Yankee Farragut Born and Reared in Dixie," Ralph Poore, *Press Register* reporter.

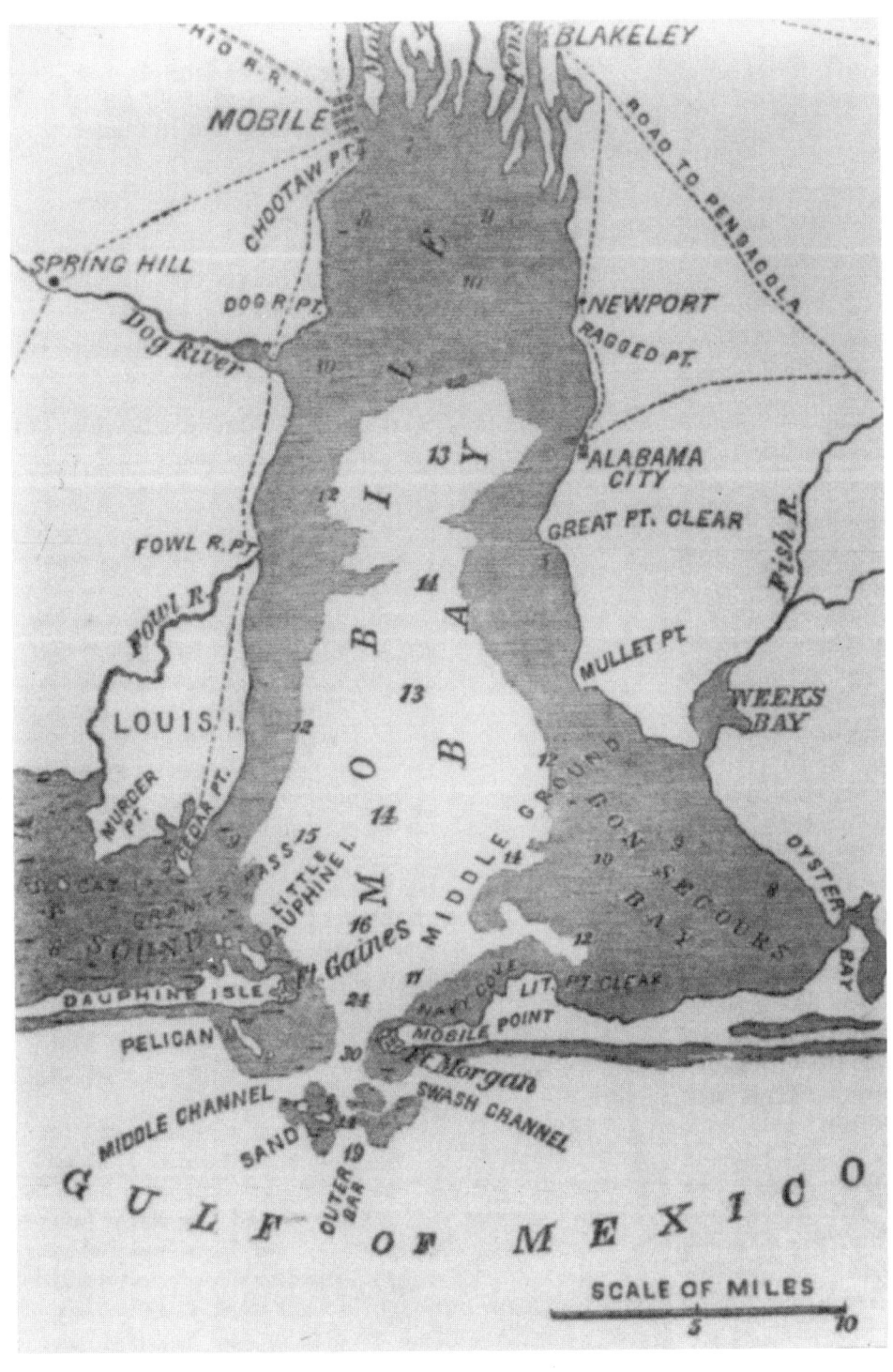

Mobile Bay
Harper's Weekly, October 26, 1861

Farragut was denied a command until 1862, possibly out of concern for his loyalty. When command came, it was immense. He was to head the western Gulf blockading squadron; his orders were to capture New Orleans and secure the Mississippi River. This he accomplished brilliantly by 1863, after which Congress created for him the title Rear Admiral. At age sixty-two, he was assigned the reduction of Mobile. He was again promoted by Congress when Mobile surrendered and was given the title Admiral.

Farragut was still active in the navy, in command of the European squadron, a year before his death in Portsmouth, New Hampshire, August 13, 1870.

Rear Admiral David G. Farragut, U.S.N., after a photograph by Brady. *Harper's Weekly*, September 17, 1864

II
The Odds

MOBILE BAY IS A LARGE, TRIANGULAR BODY OF WATER some thirty miles long, with Mobile situated at its head. The width of the Bay varies from about six miles in the upper end to about fifteen miles at its mouth.

Entrance of an enemy fleet into the Bay was made difficult by Mobile Point, a long peninsula on the eastern side jutting out into the Bay, and Dauphin Island, three miles distant from it, on the western side. There was, of course, room for an entrance on the western side between Dauphin Island and the mainland. This was, however, so shallow that only the lightest-draft vessels could get through. Thus, the entrance to the spacious Bay was narrowed to a three-mile strait and even less at shallow points. In the final analysis, then, the only entrance to the Bay for deep-draft warships was the comparatively narrow Swash Channel closely skirting the end of Mobile Point. These natural defensive advantages had been greatly strengthened by forts, floating mines,[1] and wooden pilings.

On the tip of Mobile Point stood Fort Morgan commanding the channel entrance, which passed beneath the sweep of its guns. Fort Morgan was under the command of General Richard L. Page. It was a large, star-shaped, brick fortress built in 1833 and based on a design by the French engineer Vauban (1633-1707). Besides its intended fortifications, it had been heavily reinforced with sandbags placed there by the Confederates. By the mid-nineteenth century such brick forts were obsolete and had to be covered over by dense materials such as sand, wood, or earth, which could absorb the energy of more powerful shot and shell.

---

[1] The term "torpedo" was used in the nineteenth century to describe these stationary mines.

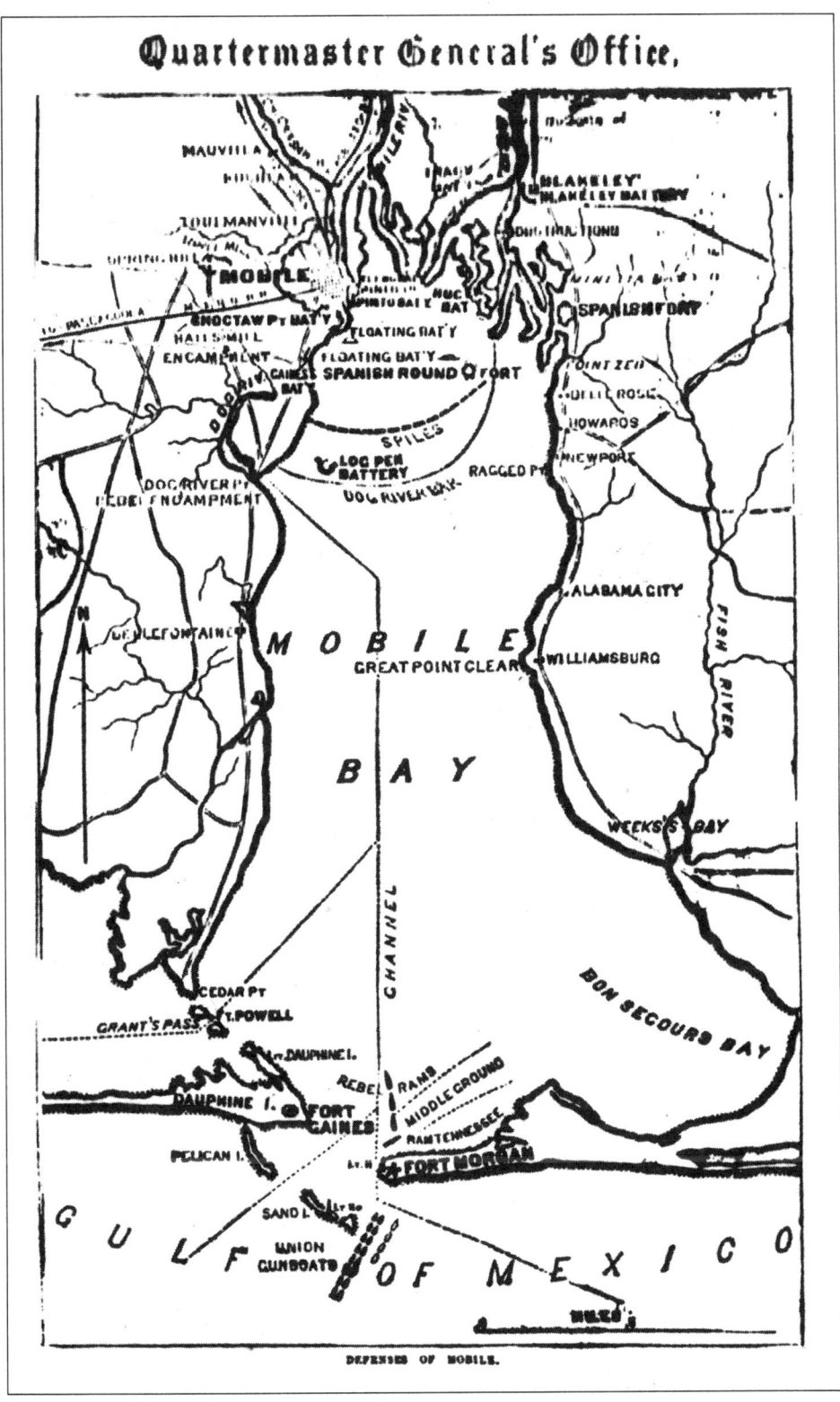

Contempary Federal Map of Mobile and its defenses.

The fort carried a fairly large battery, though none of the complement were of heavy caliber. There were in the fort:

seven 10-inch smooth bore guns,
three 8-inch smooth bore guns,
twenty-two 32-pounder smooth bore guns,
two 8-inch rifled cannon,
two 6.5-inch rifled cannon, and
four 5.82-inch rifled cannon.

Other pieces mounted outside the fort included four formidable 10-inch Columbiads, one 8-inch smoothbore and two rifled 32-pounders in the Water Battery.[2]

On the eastern point of Dauphin Island stood Fort Gaines, three miles from the tip of Mobile Point and Fort Morgan. It was of secondary importance in defending Mobile, since its guns could never effectively reach the Swash Channel. It played no important part in the battle. Its defenses consisted of some twenty-seven guns, of which three were 10-inch Columbiads and four were rifled 32-pounders; the remainder were smooth-bore 32's, 24's, and 18's.

The Confederates had also begun construction of a small battery, Fort Powell, to keep light-draft gunboats from slipping into the Bay through Grant's Pass, the shallow channel between Dauphin Island and the mainland. Fort Powell was never completed but mounted at the time of the battle a 10-inch and an 8-inch Columbiad and four rifled guns.[3]

In addition to these defenses, the Confederate army supplied a protective system of pilings and that famous Confederate

---

[2] Scharf, p. 552.
[3] Scharf, p. 553.

Fort Morgan and the Rebel fleet.
Harper's Weekly, August 20, 1864

invention, the torpedo.[4] From Fort Gaines southeasterly toward Fort Morgan, there stretched a row of ugly pilings, set low in the water, visible only at low tide, like the jaws of some fish ready to gouge the bottom out of any boat attempting to pass them. Where a sand reef formed the western edge of the channel skirting Fort Morgan, the piling left off, being supplanted by a triple row of mines[5] stretching across the channel to a red buoy just 800 feet from Fort Morgan. This left an open way of only 100 yards of safe water, which was used by friendly blockade runners. All in all, 180 mines were set out.[6] The majority of them, however, were made ineffective by the corrosive action of saltwater on the priming caps.

For a naval defense, there was in the Bay a squadron of three gunboats and the ironclad ram *Tennessee*. Commanding the squadron was Admiral Buchanan, the fearless commander of the *Merrimac*, the first ironclad, best known for its conflict with the federal ironclad, *Monitor*.[7] He was now stationed aboard his flagship, the *Tennessee*, in Mobile Bay. The three gunboats (if they can be graced by that term) were the *Selma*, the *Gaines*, and the *Morgan*. The *Gaines* and the *Morgan* were hastily built by the

---

[4] C. L. Lewis, *Admiral Franklin Buchanan* (Baltimore: The Norman, Remington Co., 1929), p. 221.

[5] Confederate mines varied widely, but most of the ones in Mobile Bay were tarred beer kegs set off by fulminate caps, or glass vials of sulphuric acid, which would break and fall on sugar, causing a spark and subsequent explosion.

[6] Scharf, p. 556.

[7] In this article the first ironclad will be called the *Merrimac*. The Confederates christened her the *Virginia;* she was built using the hull of the steamer *Merrimac*, which had burned to the waterline. After the war, Confederate sympathizers resented historians who pointedly referred to the ship as the *Merrimac*. Southerners saw this as an implication that their ironclad was not a first and unique creation. They explained that the *Merrimac* had been decommissioned, thus allowing the ship to be christened anew. But here, too, the South lost a battle.

Confederacy to aid in the Mobile defenses. They were constructed of unseasoned wood, and their engines were entirely too small for them. The *Selma* was little better, being a converted open-deck coastwise mail packet fitted with guns.[8] They were completely unarmored except for a little sheet iron around the boiler and carried these guns:

Morgan: two 7-inch rifles and four 32-pounders;
Gaines: one 8-inch rifle and five 32-pounders;
Selma: three 8-inch old-fashioned Paixhan shell guns and one ancient, smooth-bore 33-pounder.

The ironclad *Tennessee,* though called by the Yankees a "monster" and "the most formidable vessel afloat," was, because of lack of finances and materials, not so terrible after all. She was built in the general Confederate class of ironclads, somewhat like the *Merrimac,* essentially a sunken hull with an iron casement or boxlike enclosure projecting from it, with a cannon battery placed inside. The Confederates, knowing that an ironclad was necessary for the defense of the Bay, had done everything in their power to expedite its completion.

> ... She was built at the naval station at Selma, in the winter of 1863-64, and so expeditiously was the work done upon her that when her keel was laid, some of the timbers to be used in her were still standing and much of what was to be her plating was ore in the mines.[9]

For a nation in the state the Confederacy found itself at the close of the war, the building of so complex a machine, even with its deficiencies, was remarkable. It is estimated that she cost

---

[8] Scharf, p. 556.
[9] Scharf, p. 555.

the South $883,880.[10] This is a small estimate, however, as much of her labor was never paid for. The patriotic men of Selma worked through the whole day, and at night fires and torches lit the labor of the crews working over the huge hulk.

The "Tennessee" was 209 feet in length, with an extreme beam of 48 feet and carried her battery in a casemate or shield amidships 79 feet long and 29 feet wide, inside dimensions. Her frame was composed of yellow pine beams, 13 inches thick, set close together vertically and planked with 5 1/2 inches of yellow pine in vertical courses. Within, the yellow pine frames were sheathed with 2 1/2 inches of oak. The outer walls of the casemates were inclined at an angle of 45 degrees from the deck and on this 25 inches of wood backing was laid plate armor, which was 6 inches thick on the forward wall, and elsewhere 5 inches thick, and was fastened to the wood with bolts 1 1/4 inches in diameter that went entirely through the wall and were secured by nuts and washers on the inside. The outside deck was plated with 2 inches of iron. A curious arrangement of the casemate was that its sloping sides were carried down two feet below the waterline, and then reversed at the same angle so that they met the hull seven feet under water. This projection was carried out around the bow, where it was fashioned into a spur or ram. The pilot house stood on the forward edge of the casemate and was in fact made by building it up some three feet. There were ten ports, two on each side, three forward and three aft, so arranged that the pivot guns could be fought in broadside, sharp on the bow and quarter and on a direct line with the keel, but the ship never had more than six guns. At each end she carried a Brooke $7\,1/_8$-inch rifled gun on pivots, capable of throwing a solid projectile of 110 pounds weight. There were also four Brooke 6-inch rifles in broad-

[10] *Official Records of the Union and Confederate Navies in the War of the Rebellion,* published under the direction of C. J. Bonaparte, Series I, Vol. 21 (Washington Government Printing Office: Charles W. Stewart, 1906), p. 567.

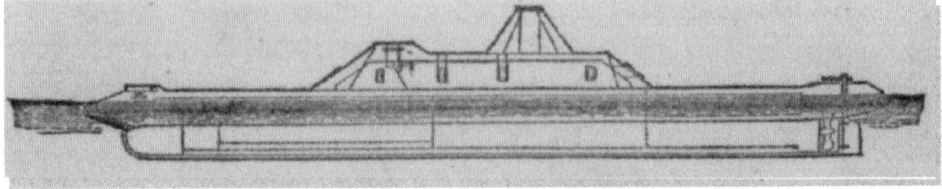

Above and top right: Illustration of the *Tennessee* from Scharf's *History of the Confederate States Navy.*

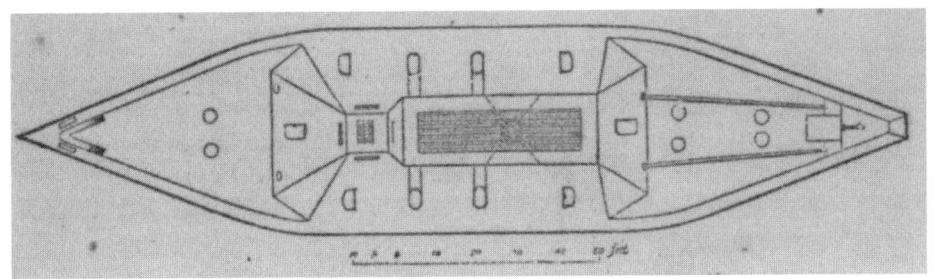

side, each firing a 95-pound solid shot. . . . One avoidable defect was the manner of constructing the port shutters which revolved upon a pivot and were fatally apt to be jammed in an engagement. Another and greater blunder was that the rudder chains were exposed upon the after deck, where they were at any moment liable to be shot away. Of the defects that could not be avoided the worst was her lack of speed. Her engines were not built for the ship, but were taken from the high-pressure river steamboat 'Alonzo Child'; and though on her trial trip, in March, 1864, her speed was set down at 8 nautical miles per hour she could not make more than six with her battery, ammunition and fuel on board.[11]

Such she was, in all a fighting machine of which the South could be justly proud.

Nevertheless, the Northern fleet, riding at anchor outside the Bay in the choppy Gulf, was a superior adversary for the meager Confederate squadron. The Northern fleet was mainly wooden screw-steamers, but it had four monitor-class ironclads, any of which was the better of the *Tennessee* in construction, engines, and equipment. Some post-war northern history books made as much over the *Tennessee* and her sister ships as the patriotic Southern newspapers of that day did, which confuses the issue. One cannot intelligently evaluate the battle unless one realizes the huge odds in ships and guns the Federal fleet held over the Confederate fleet.

...Commodore Foxhall A. Parker, of the U. S. Navy states in his paper upon the battle of Mobile Bay, read before the Military Historical Society of Massachusetts, December 10th, 1877, that their (the Federal fleet's) total weight of metal was 14,246 pounds, and that they

[11] Scharf, pp. 553-54.

threw at a broadside 9,288 pounds. The total weight of metal that could be thrown from all the 'Tennessee's guns at one discharge was but 600 pounds, while 900 pounds is a large allowance for a single round from the three other Confederate craft. Thus it will be seen that the difference between the concentrated fire of the Federal fleet, and that of Buchanan's squadron, was nearly ten pounds to one in favor of the former. Each of Farragut's ships had been built for the naval service, and they constituted the pick of the fighting force of the U. S. government. His Monitors were the most powerful ironclads that had been built. The 'Tecumseh' and the 'Manhattan' were armored with ten inches of iron on their turrets, as against the six inches of the 'Tennessee's casemate, and each carried in her turret two 15-inch guns, the heaviest that in those days had been put on shipboard.

The 'Chickasaw' and 'Winnebago' were double turret monitors, clad in eight and one-half inches of iron, and firing from each turret two 11-inch guns. The 'Hartford', 'Brooklyn', and 'Richmond' were second-class wooden screw-steamers carrying nine-inch Dahlgren guns, and 100-pounder Parrott rifles, and these very effective pieces of ordnance were common throughout the fleet, even the smallest ships mounting at least one nine or eleven-inch gun in addition to the most approved form of rifled cannon and howitzers. There were few such obsolete guns on board any of them as the thirty-two pounders of the 'Gaines', 'Morgan', and 'Selma'. By far the most valuable guns in possession of the Confederates were the Brooke rifles, which were manufactured at Richmond, under the direction of their inventor, Commander John M. Brooke, of the C. S. Navy; but the largest of them were but little over eight inches calibre, his facilities being too restricted to allow him to turn out pieces like the eleven and fifteen-inch cannon that the Federals placed so great a reliance upon.[12]

It has been estimated that, in fact, Admiral Buchanan had only 14 heavy calibre guns with which to contend against 113 of the enemy.[13] Such were the odds for the coming battle.

The only advantages that the South had were the fort and the mines. The North had an unlimited potential fleet, quantity and quality of arms, and the advantage of choosing the time of attack. The Confederates fully realized that they could not begin an offensive.

[12] Scharf, p. 559 (footnote).
[13] Lewis, p. 225.

Admiral Franklin Buchanan, an engraving from Scharf's History of the Confederate States Navy.

III

A Battle in Four Acts

Act One: Balanced to Partners

ADMIRAL FARRAGUT COULD STAND UPON THE DECK OF HIS flagship, the *Hartford*, and look inland to Mobile Bay. He could see little clusters of boats and men driving piling and laying torpedoes. He could see the huge ram *Tennessee* steaming slowly about in front of Fort Morgan. He realized that every minute wasted would probably mean more lives lost, and he wanted more than anything else to pass the fort and conquer the Confederate squadron. Only one thing was holding him up: the arrival of the single turret monitor *Tecumseh*. He did not trust his wooden ships and the monitors he already had in a battle with the *Tennessee*. The *Tecumseh* and her sister the *Manhattan* had the fifteen-inch guns, and it was thought that with these they could disable the *Tennessee*.

Farragut had conceived his entire battle plan in early July. He wanted the wooden ships to go in lashed in pairs, a plan he had used in battle before, so that if one was disabled by the fire of Fort Morgan, its consort could tow it past the range of the fort. They were to fire as fast as their guns could be brought to bear, use short fuses for shell and shrapnel, and fire grape shot at 300 or 400 yards.[1]

Toward the end of July, actual battle preparations began. In a general order to the fleet, Farragut advised:

> Strip your vessels and prepare for the conflict. Send down all your superfluous spars and spare rigging. Put up the splinter-nets on the starboard side, and barricade the wheel and steersman with sails and hammock. Lay chains or sandbags on the deck, over the machinery

---

[1] Scharf, p. 558.

to resist a plunging fire. Hang the sheet chains over the side, or make any other arrangements your ingenuity may suggest . . . .[2]

Great preparations were made for the most difficult part of the battle, the passing of Fort Morgan. The wooden ship *Richmond,* for example, had a barricade from the port bow around the starboard side to the port quarter built of 3,000 sandbags. Chain cables were hung over the sides to protect the engines and boilers. Even the coal in the coal-bunkers was shifted so that it would catch shot coming in toward the boilers.[3]

Amid this activity, Farragut impatiently awaited the arrival of the *Tecumseh.* On August 3, 1864, about 2,000 men under Major-General Gordon Granger landed under cover of a flotilla of light-draft gunboats a few miles down Dauphin Island to invade Fort Gaines.[4] This army land attack had been another factor in holding up the battle for Farragut, and he now felt more ready to go in. Late in the evening, August 4, 1864, the *Tecumseh* steamed into Farragut's fleet. Farragut decided to begin the battle on the morning of the next day.

For the men on the Yankee ships, the night before the battle was, at most, a sober one. The first hours of the night were taken up with writing letters home or instructions in case of death. It was a quiet, calm night, and the lights aboard each waiting ship told of a group of sailors quietly sitting around swapping yarns or singing, then, after a final smoke, going to bed for a little sleep, if possible.

Toward midnight, a fog arose and hampered the preparation of the vessels that began a little after three in the morning. The ships presented a strange scene as they "balanced to partners."

---

[2] Edward Shippen, *Naval Battles of America* (Philadelphia: P. W. Ziegler Co., 1905), p. 223.
[3] Scharf, p. 559.
[4] Scharf, p. 558.

Their outlines loomed here and there like phantom ships as they lashed themselves side by side in the white fog.[5]

The admiral had arisen about three in the morning, and weather conditions satisfying him, he ordered preparations to go ahead.[6] Because he chose the offensive, he could choose the conditions, which he did, much to his advantage. A four-knot flood tide was running to help his ships by the fort, and the westerly breeze would blow the smoke of battle onto the gunners at Fort Morgan.[7]

The line was formed, and at 5:45 in the morning, Friday, August 5, 1864, the slow procession began.[8] The fog had lifted; the day was clear and sunny. The Federal fleet, going to oppose the fort and the four ships and the torpedoes, was then the largest grouped navel force on the face of the earth.[9]

The order in which the Federal fleet steamed into the bay:

Monitors—Starboard Column

Tecumseh	1,034 tons	two guns, Comr. T. A. M. Craven
Manhattan	1,034 tons	two guns, Comr. S. W. A. Nicholson
Winnebago	970 tons	four guns, Comr. Thomas Stephens
Chickasaw	970 tons	four guns, Lt.-Comr. G. H. Perkins

---

[5] Robert Underwood Johnson, *Battles and Leaders of the Civil War* (New York: The Century Co., 1887), pp. 385-86.

[6] Jim Dan Hill, *Sea Dog of the Sixties* (Minneapolis: The University of Minnesota Press, 1935), p. 50.

[7] F. Green and H. Frost, *Some Famous Sea Fights* (New York and London: The Century Co., 1927), p. 214.

[8] Johnson, p. 386.

[9] Scharf, p. 559

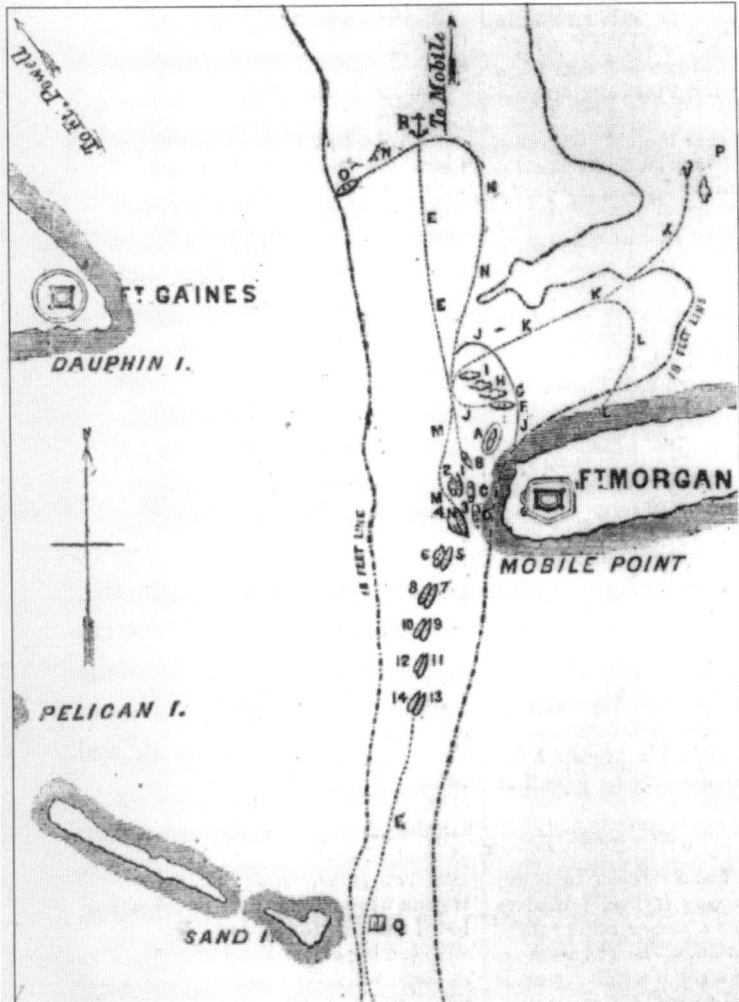

Plan of the Battle of August 5, 1864.

Harper's Weekly, September 24, 1864
This is one of the earliest diagrams of the Battle. I was taken from eye-witness accounts and drawn by a *Harper's* artist.

Wooden Vessels	**Ironclads**	
1. Brookyn	A. Tecumseh, sunk by torpedo	J. Course of Ram
2. Octorora		
3. Hartford	B. Manhattan	K. Retreat of Rebel Wooden Vessels
4. Metacomet	C. Winnebago	
5. Richmond	D. Chickasaw	L. Morgan and Gaines's course toward Fort Morgan
6. Port Royal		
7. Lackawanna	E. Course of Union Fleet	M. Hartford turning out for Brooklyn to back
8. Seminole		
9. Monongahela	**Rebel Vessels**	N. Course taken by Ram during second attack
10. Kennebec	F. Ram Tennessee	
11. Ossipee	G. Morgan	O. Ram surrendered
12. Itasca	H. Gaines	P. Selma surrendered to Metacomet
13. Oneida	I. Selma	
14. Galena		Q. Formed line; read prayers
		R. Union Fleet anchored

Wooden Ships—Port Column

Brooklyn	2,070 tons	twenty-four guns, Capt. James Alden
Octorara	829 tons	six guns, Lt.-Comr. Chas. A. Greene
Hartford	1,900 tons	twenty-one guns, Capt. Percival Drayton
Metacomet	974 tons	six guns, Lt.-Comr. Jas. E. Jouett
Richmond	1,929 tons	twenty guns, Capt. Thornton Jenkins
Port Royal	805 tons	six guns, Lt.-Comr. B. Gherardi
Lackawanna	1,533 tons	eight guns, Capt. John B. Marchand
Seminole	801 tons	eight guns, Comr. Edward Donaldson
Monongahela	1,378 tons	eight guns, Comr. J. H. Strong
Kennebec	507 tons	five guns, Lt.-Comr. W. P. McCann
Ossipee	1,240 tons	eleven guns, Comr. William Leroy
Itasca	507 tons	six guns, Lt.-Comr. Geo. Brown
Oneida	1,032 tons	nine guns, Comr. J. R. M. Mullany
Galena	738 tons	ten guns, Lt.-Comr. Clark Wells[10]

Eleven other light-draft ships participated in the battle, five of them bombarding little Fort Powell while the other six lay outside Fort Morgan in the Gulf, supposedly to draw the fire of the Confederate guns. They never came in close enough to carry out this plan, however. They played little part in the actual battle and are only mentioned to create a full picture.[11]

The *Tecumseh* led the monitor column, which was to run closer to the fort to draw fire from the wooden vessels. It was known that shot from Fort Morgan would do little harm to the iron turrets of the monitors.

The *Brooklyn* led the wooden ships because she had a device for picking up torpedoes on her bow and four chase guns for firing ahead.[12] It was also known that the Confederates would naturally attempt to sink the admiral's flagship, so the *Hartford* was placed in a more protected position rather than leading the attack.

---

[10] Scharf, p. 559.
[11] Lewis, frontispiece.
[12] Johnson, p. 383.

On the Confederate side, the intent of the enemy was immediately known, as it had been expected for some days. The Confederate sailors were not too sorry to see the attack come, as can be seen by this eye-witness report.

> "We had been very uncomfortable for many weeks in our berths on board the 'Tennessee', " wrote Fleet Surgeon Daniel B. Conrad, "in consequence of the prevailing rains wetting the decks, and the terrible moist, hot atmosphere, simulating that oppressiveness which precedes a tornado. It was, therefore, impossible to sleep inside; besides, from the want of properly cooked food, and the continuous wetting of the decks at night, the officers and the men were rendered desperate. We knew that the impending action would soon be determined one way or the other and everyone looked forward to it with a positive feeling of relief. I had been sleeping on the deck of the admiral's cabin for two or three nights, when at daybreak on the 5th of August, the old quartermaster came down the ladder, rousing us up with his gruff voice, saying: 'Admiral, the officer of the deck bids me report that the enemy's fleet is under way.' Jumping up, still half asleep, we came on deck, and sure enough, there was the enemy heading for the 'passage' past the fort. The grand old admiral, of sixty years, with his countenance rigid and stern, showing a determination for battle in every line, then gave his only order, 'Get under way, Captain Johnston; head for the leading vessel of the enemy, and fight each one as they pass.' "[13]

Admiral Buchanan called his men together and spoke to them. It was a stern message, and he meant what he said:

> Now men, the enemy is coming, and I want you to do your duty; and you shall not have it to say when you leave this vessel that you were not near enough to the enemy, for I will meet them, and then you can fight them alongside of their own ships; and if I fall, lay me on one side and go on with the fight, and never mind me—but whip and sink the Yankees or fight until you sink yourselves, but do not surrender.[14]

[13] Lewis, p. 226.
[14] Lewis, p. 228.

Buchanan then moved his ship up to a position in the middle of the channel just a little outside the line of torpedoes. The *Selma, Gaines,* and *Morgan* took up a position to the side and a little to the rear of the flagship *Tennessee* where they might direct a raking fire on the advancing ships, fore and aft.[15]

Act Two: The Narrow Channel

At exactly 6:47 A.M., the great gun of the *Tecumseh* opened the battle with a shot at Fort Morgan. Some twenty minutes later, when the ships were in closer range, Fort Morgan opened fire on the foremost of the fleet.[16]

> By a quarter-past seven o'clock the action had become general. Farragut's ships pouring their broadsides into Fort Morgan, which responded with so much energy that a dense cloud of smoke had already settled down upon the bay, above which loomed the masts and spars of the Federal fleet, while it was incessantly lit up with flashes of the guns.[17]

Still Admiral Buchanan reserved his fire, and the *Tennessee* lay quietly while the monitor *Tecumseh* moved slowly toward her. It was the prearranged plan for the monitors, especially the *Tecumseh,* to dispatch the *Tennessee* if possible, and then follow the fleet on up the Bay.[18] Buchanan knew this and was waiting quietly for the coming conflict. The admiral had relayed an order to Lieutenant Wharton of the first division of the *Tennessee* not to fire until the vessels were in actual contact. As Wharton heard the

---

[15] Lewis, p. 227.
[16] Lewis, p. 226.
[17] Scharf, p. 560.
[18] An order to the monitors *Tecumseh* and *Manhattan* in a letter written by Farragut on August 4, 1864.

command, he tautened the lockstring of the bow gun in his fingers and tensely awaited the slowly advancing *Tecumseh*. Simultaneously, Buchanan ordered the *Tennessee* to be moved a little to the west and somewhat behind the deadly row of torpedoes. This placed the line of torpedoes between the *Tecumseh* and *Tennessee*.[19]

Captain T. A. M. Craven of the *Tecumseh* looked through the slit of his tiny, smoke-filled conning tower and, seeing the action of the *Tennessee*, changed his course and headed directly toward her. Some say he felt that there was not enough room for him to pass on the eastward side, and some say he was not aware of the danger in which he was placing himself. It is known, however, that he began to turn and move his monitor toward the *Tennessee* and the string of torpedoes.

Meanwhile, the wooden ship, *Brooklyn*, moving faster than the starboard column of monitors, came abreast of the fort and nearly alongside the rear-most monitor.[20] Captain Alden of the *Brooklyn* saw the *Tecumseh* head toward the *Tennessee* and subsequently right across his bows. He wondered if the entire monitor column was going to be led across in front of him. At the same time, a cry went up from the *Brooklyn* that "black objects" were sighted ahead in the water.[21] Across his brain flashed the thought of torpedoes—those deadly explosives that required no marksmanship or guns but that could sink a ship in seconds. Panic gripped him, and he made a terrible blunder. He halted his ship and begin backing, spinning with the tide, and signaling with army signals to the *Hartford:* "The monitors are right ahead. We cannot go on without passing them. What shall we do?"

[19] Scharf, p. 561.
[20] Johnson, p. 387.
[21] Hill, p. 54.

Farragut's Fleet Passing the Forts and Obstructions at the Entrance of Mobile Bay.
August 5, 1864

Harper's Weekly, September 3, 1864

Farragut quickly answered, "Order the monitors ahead and go on."[22] It was a desperate moment. The ships were beginning to pile up behind the stalled *Brooklyn,* and the almost stationary gunboats presented an excellent target to the Confederate gunners at Fort Morgan. Their shots were beginning to take effect.

The *Tecumseh,* having stalled the *Brooklyn,* was now, you remember, heading toward the *Tennessee,* There was a momentary silence as the two Goliaths drew nearer. The two were within a hundred yards of each other when a muffled roar like thunder was heard and

> ...a column of water like a fountain springing from the sea shot up beside the Federal monitor; she lurched violently, her head settled, her stern went up into the air so that her revolving screw could plainly be seen, and then the waves closed over her .... [23]

The action on both sides stopped as the men stood stunned at the suddenness of the disappearance of the huge ship. Where there had been a ship, there was now, only 30 seconds later, a small knot of men struggling in the waves. One hundred and fourteen men had drowned instantly. Among the dead was Commander Craven, who, by his disobedience of Farragut, had caused the loss of his ship and his life.[24]

Pilot Collins of the *Tecumseh* afterward told of the heroic death of Craven. As the ship was sinking, Pilot Collins and Commander Craven raced to the ladder leading to the top of the

---

[22] Johnson, p. 388.
[23] Scharf, p. 561.
[24] General Orders, no. 11: There are certain black buoys placed by the enemy from the piles on the west side of the channel across it toward Ford Morgan. It being understood that there are torpedoes and other obstructions between the buoys the vessels will take care to pass to the eastward of the easternmost buoy, which is clear of all obstructions .... D. G. Farragut, Rear-Admiral.

Destruction of the monitor Tecumseh by a rebel torpedo in Mobile Bay, August 5, 1864 [Sketched by Robert Weir.]

Harper's Weekly, September 10, 1864

turret. The gallant Craven stepped back and said, "After you, Pilot." "There was nothing after me," said the pilot, "when I reached the upmost round of the ladder, the vessel seemed to drop from under me."[25] So went the *Tecumseh;* it lies there today, slowly rusting in the bottom of the Bay. A buoy marking the

---

[25] Lewis, p. 229.

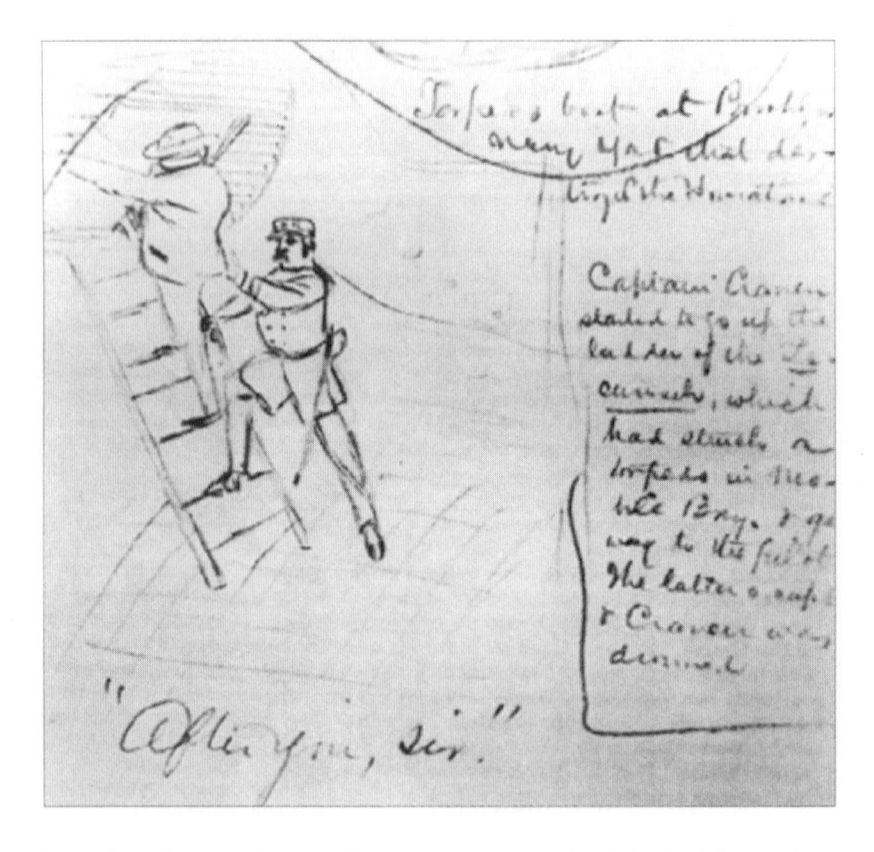

Craven's gallantry, *After you, Sir*, a contemporary sketch in the Library of Congress. A reproduction is found in Caldwell Delany's *Confederate Mobile*.

location may be seen a few hundred yards off the concrete pier at Fort Morgan. A small boat was put out from the wooden ship *Metacomet* to pick up the few survivors. General Page in Fort Morgan with true gallantry said to his officers, "Pass the order not to fire on that boat; she is saving drowning men."[26]

The *Brooklyn* still remained immobile. She had sheered around now and presented her whole side to the batteries of Fort Morgan. The Confederate gunboats were firing upon the whole fleet, and Farragut found himself in the direst straits imaginable. He then received a message from the *Brooklyn* announcing the sinking of the *Tecumseh*—a rather needless announcement, for everyone of both fleets was aware of the fact by now, if he had not seen it himself. Farragut sent an urgent message to the *Brooklyn* to "go on." This was not obeyed, and the whole fleet lay open to a raking fire from the Confederates, while they could hardly bring a gun to bear.

The *Hartford,* in particular, received a galling punishment. The decks were literally running blood from the scuppers and, as one officer described it, "mangled fragments of humanity were scattered across the decks." One poor gunner was decapitated by a solid shot coming through the bows. The thickness of the rain of shot and shells upon the ships is made apparent by the fate of a sailor on the *Hartford*. He lost both legs by the passing of a solid shot, and as he fell to the deck, raising his arms in agony, they, too, were carried away by a cannon ball.[27] Another eye witness said: "The batteries of our ships were almost silent, while the whole of Mobile Point was a living flame."

It was obvious that something had to be done. The clear-thinking Farragut acted decisively and saved the day. He had, as

---

[26] Green and Frost, p. 222.
[27] Johnson, p. 389.

the battle progressed, climbed up the rigging to see over the smoke. He was now just beneath the main top, the pilot standing over his head. The captain of the *Hartford,* seeing Farragut in the rigging, feared shrapnel or a splinter might strike him, causing him to fall to the deck. To avert this, he sent the quartermaster to him with a small cord, which he tied around the admiral's waist. He shouted to the pilot above him and asked if there was enough water for him to pass around the *Brooklyn.* The pilot said that there was. Farragut then said, "I will take the lead." He ordered the *Hartford* full speed ahead and her escort, the *Metacomet,* to back full speed with her paddlewheels. This pivoted the two ships on their heels, swinging them clear of the motionless *Brooklyn* to allow the flagship to take the lead.[28] It had been only ten minutes between this decision and the balking of the *Brooklyn,* but in this time, the Confederate squadron and the fort had taken quite a toll in lives and damage.[29]

Much was later written in the popular press about Farragut going into battle "lashed to the masthead." This was a great exaggeration. The image, sometimes accurately depicted, sometimes not, appeared in numerous engravings, oil paintings, and in a stained glass window installed in the U.S. Naval Academy in Annapolis, Maryland.[30]

It cannot be proven that Farragut uttered "Damn the torpedoes, full speed ahead!" No first hand reports, memoirs, or press accounts mention this expression. The less dramatic "I will take the lead" means the same thing but lacks the dramatic force of the cry that can only be traced to later sources.

---

[28] Hill, p. 55.
[29] Johnson, p. 391 (footnote).
[30] This was the war between brothers. The Union man Farragut of Tennessee and Mississippi attacked the Confederate man Buchanan of Maryland. Farragut's window was installed in the Naval Academy where Buchanan had served as the first superintendent.

The action in passing the *Brooklyn* took the courageous Farragut right over the line of torpedoes, but none of them exploded, though men in the hold heard some of the primers snap.

The *Tennessee* now found herself with an opportunity to sink the *Hartford* as she passed the *Brooklyn*. Wharton himself, the officer of the forward division, aimed the piece and fired it. He congratulated himself, he later said, upon the sinking of the Federal flagship. The shell did explode and put a hole in the *Hartford,* but it was above the waterline.[31]

The plan of battle and the battle line itself were now restored by Farragut's actions. Fort Morgan hulled each ship repeatedly, but the precautions taken before the battle (sandbags, chains, etc.) saved each one from being mechanically disabled, except for the *Oneida*. Her starboard boiler was exploded and two of her guns were knocked off their mounts. She was towed past the fort by her consort, the *Galena*.[32] Then the wisdom of lashing the ships together was proved.

Act Three: Four against Seventeen

By this time, the Federal fleet was almost past Fort Morgan. The captains of the Confederate fleet realized that it was up to them alone to turn back the enemy.

As the *Hartford* passed over the torpedo line and took the lead, the three small Confederate gunboats ran close down upon

---

[31] Scharf, p. 562.
[32] Scharf, p. 563.

the starboard bow of the flagship and sent a rain of shot and shell into her. They kept this fire up, using mostly the stern guns and keeping from 700 to 1,000 yards ahead of the flagship. One shot from the *Selma* struck her forward gun and killed ten men who were serving it. The force of exploding shells threw splinters of deck wood and human limbs onto the deck of her consort ship, the *Metacomet*.[33]

At the same time, the *Tennessee* had attempted to ram the *Hartford*. But the *Tennessee* was clumsy and Buchanan missed his mark. Realizing that he could never hope to chase and catch the *Hartford*, he left her to the three gunboats and stood on down the Bay to meet the remainder of the Federal fleet, which had now extricated itself from the confusion and was slowly steaming up the Bay.

As to what happened when the *Tennessee* met the first ship, Admiral Jenkins of the *Richmond* writes:

> As the "Tennessee" approached, everyone on board the "Richmond" supposed that she would ram the "Brooklyn"; that, we thought would be our opportunity, for if she struck the "Brooklyn" the concussion would throw her port side across our path, and being so near to us, she would not have time to "straighten up", and we would strike her fairly and squarely, and most likely sink her.
>
> The guns were loaded with solid shot and heaviest powder charge; the forecastle gun's crew were ordered to get their small arms and fire into her gun-ports; and as previously determined, if we came in collision at any time, the orders were to throw gun-charges of powder in bags from the fore and main yard-arms down her smokestack (or at least try to do so). To our great surprise, she sheered off from the

---

[33] Scharf, p. 563.

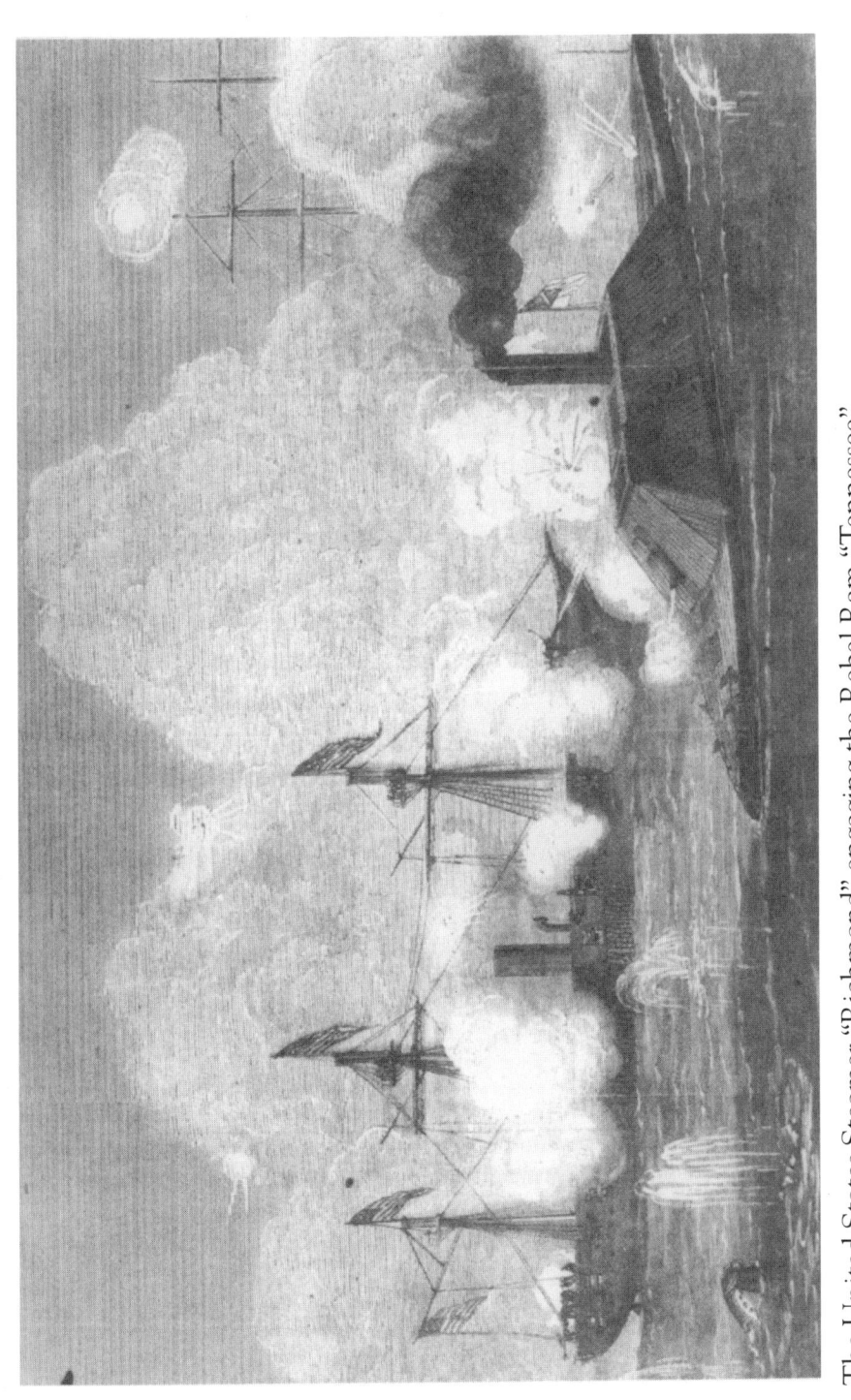

The United States Steamer "Richmond" engaging the Rebel Ram "Tennessee" August 5, 1864. – Sketched by Robert Weir.

Harper's Weekly, September 10, 1864

"Brooklyn", and at about one hundred yards put two shot or shells through and through the "Brooklyn's" sides (as reported) doing much damage. . . .[34]

Captain Story of the sloop-of-war *Monongahela* saw that the fire from the other ships was bounding off the *Tennessee* like so many tennis balls. His ship being fitted with a steel beak, he attempted to ram her. By an adroit movement, Admiral Buchanan avoided the direct blow, and, in so doing, he rasped along the quarter of the *Kennebec*, the *Monongahela's* consort, and lodged a shell in her berth deck, doing quite a bit of damage. Next up, he faced the *Ossipee*, into which he fired a few shots. Then, in a clever maneuver, he swung in a tight circle around the stern of the crippled *Oneida*, into which he discharged two full broadsides, which disabled two guns, carried away much of the lower tackle, and shot off Commander Mullany's arm.[35] He had pitted his one ship against eight and came out of the affair entirely unhurt.[36]

The *Tennessee* left the *Oneida*, the last of the line, at 8:40 A.M. About that time, Fort Morgan ceased fire, the ships now being past the range of her guns. She had expended 491 rounds.[37]

At the same time, the *Hartford* found herself well up into the Bay and was now suffering chiefly from the running battle with the three gunboats. As soon, however, as Farragut found himself past the guns of Fort Morgan, he allowed his ships to unlash themselves. The speedier chase boats, such as the *Metacomet* and *Itasca*, set out at once to run down the gunboats.[38] The remainder of the fleet lower down the Bay, seeing what was being done up ahead, also cast off, all the faster ships joining the chase.[39] The

---

[34] Johnson, p. 393.
[35] Scharf, p. 564.
[36] Buchanan could have done much better here had his gun primers not been defective. He suffered throughout the battle because of the misfire of his guns.
[37] Green and Frost, p. 224.
[38] Scharf, p. 564.
[39] Johnson, p. 393.

Confederate captains fully realized that they could never outdistance the Federal craft, but, regardless, they continued to fire from their stern guns and slowly retreated. The *Gaines* was the first to go. She received a solid shot, then a percussion shell at the same spot below the waterline. The resulting hole caused the magazine to flood, and she began to sink. The starboard cannon battery was run over to the port side in an attempt to raise the hole above water. When this failed, she was turned about and run ashore near Fort Morgan. Her men left her quietly, and, with deep regret, Captain Bennet set the torch to her. The *Morgan* escaped to Fort Morgan unharmed and that night made an escape through the Federal fleet to Mobile. The *Metacomet* chased the running *Selma*, coming within range about nine o'clock. Lt. P.U. Murphy had shifted all gunners to the stern. The *Selma* refused to surrender, and the two ships engaged in a short and bloody battle. When Executive Officer J. H. Comstock and four other men had been killed, Murphy realized the futility of the ship's actions and struck the flag.[40]

Act Four: The *Tennessee* Alone

Meanwhile, the *Tennessee* had anchored under the guns of Fort Morgan to give her men a rest and let them have some breakfast. The heat in the casemate made eating impossible, so the men stood around outside eating and talking. Buchanan himself "stumped" up and down the top deck in thought.[41] About fifteen

---

[40] Johnson, p. 566.
[41] His lameness was caused by a leg wound suffered in the *Merrimac's* battle against the wooden ships *Congress* and *Cumberland*.

minutes later, he turned to Captain Johnston and issued the terse command: "Follow them up, Johnston; we can't let them off that way." Suppressed exclamations were heard from the crew when they saw the iron prow of the ship turned toward the distant enemy.

Surgeon Conrad dared to ask the admiral if he was really going into the fleet. "I am, sir!" he replied. Conrad turned away dumbfounded and whispered to a nearby officer, "Well, we'll never come out of there whole." Buchanan unfortunately heard this. He turned, his face as gray and hard as the iron sides of the *Tennessee,* and said sharply, "That's my lookout, sir!"[42]

Buchanan was entering the fight again with only one ship against an entire fleet, any of whose three ironclads was the equal of his own. The Federal fleet had also anchored some four miles up the Bay, and her sailors were busily at work swabbing the blood from her decks and collecting the dead, while the cooks prepared breakfast.[43] Farragut had planned to go back and fight the *Tennessee* after his men had breakfasted and rested.[44] He was shocked to learn that she was now coming, and said to himself, "I did not think old Buchanan was such a fool."[45]

A general order was at once sent out to the fleet, "Attack the ram . . . at full speed."[46] Special orders were also sent to the speedier ships *Monongahela* and *Lackawanna* to "run down the ram." The two ships at once set out, with the *Monongahela* taking the lead. The *Monongahela* rammed the *Tennessee* first; the blow was an oblique one and no harm was done, although the shock knocked men from their feet on both vessels.[47] The *Monongahela*

---

[42] Lewis, p. 234.
[43] Johnson, p. 359.
[44] Lewis, p. 246.
[45] Hill, p. 57.
[46] J. P. Frothingham, *Sea Fighters from Drake to Farragut* (New York: Scribner's Sons, 1927), p 393.
[47] Scharf, p. 567.

suffered the most damage. The shock had carried away her entire prow and cutwater.

All this time, the *Tennessee* was firing as fast as she could load her guns; in fact, she hardly had to aim her guns, so numerous were the ships around her. The next ship to strike was the *Lackawanna,* who struck such a blow that the huge ram was swung violently around, listing to port; she speedily righted herself, while the *Lackawanna*'s entire stem was stove in for several feet below the waterline.[48] As the two ships parted, the *Lackawanna* swung alongside the ram, and the *Tennessee* fired two shots through and through her. Of this contact, Captain Marchand of the *Lackawanna* dryly remarked:

> A few of the enemy were seen through their ports, who were using most opprobrious language. Our marines opened on them with muskets: even a spitoon and a holystone were thrown at them from our deck, which drove them away.[49]

The *Tennessee* did not come out of the encounter entirely unscathed; she was somewhat loosened up, and upon sounding the pumps, it was found she was leaking at the rate of six inches an hour.[50] At this point, the *Tennessee* headed directly toward the *Hartford,* which was coming toward her. The two flagships bore down upon each other bow to bow. Buchanan realized that to strike her then would ram his ship so far into the wooden ship that they both would sink before he could extricate himself. Therefore, as much as he wanted to sink the *Hartford,* he turned slightly and

---

[48] Scharf, p. 567.
[49] Willis J. Abbot, *The Naval History of the United States* (New York: Dodd Mead and Company, 1896), pp. 979-80.
[50] Scharf, p. 568.

the two great ships struck, port bow to port bow. The *Tennessee* fired but one gun, due to defective primers.[51] The *Hartford*, however, gave her a full broadside at ten feet. The shot had about as much effect as hail on a tin roof.[52] The *Hartford* now swung around the *Tennessee* and came in again to strike her amidships. The *Lackawanna,* too, was charging in, and unfortunately plowed straight into the *Hartford*'s side, making a huge hole. By extreme luck, the hole was a few inches above the waterline, thus saving the Yankee fleet from the embarrassment of sinking its own flagship. The two ships separated and charged in again. By another unfortunate bit of steermanship, the *Hartford* again got into the *Lackawanna*'s path. Farragut had not gone into Mobile Bay to sink his own ships, and by now was in a towering rage. He shouted to the signalman, "Can you say 'For God's sake' by signal?" "Yes, sir," was the reply. "Then say to the *Lackawanna,* 'For God's sake, get out of our way and anchor!' " To add to the confusion, in his haste the nervous signalman struck Farragut over the head with the end of his signal staff. Fortunately, this hasty message, given in anger, was never received. The signalman in the foretop of the *Lackawanna* had just received the first five words of the message when the ship's flag blew around him so that he was unable to read the conclusion of the message.[53] By this time, the ponderous monitors had arrived on the scene of the battle and began to maneuver against the *Tennessee.*

  The monitor *Chickasaw* took up a position about fifty yards from the *Tennessee*'s stern and began pelting her with steel-headed projectiles from her 11-inch guns.[54] Up to this time, the

---

[51] This shot killed five men and wounded eight others.
[52] Green and Frost, p. 227.
[53] Johnson, p. 397.
[54] Charles Lee Lewis, *Famous American Naval Officers* (Boston: L. C. Page and Company, 1924), p. 246.

Farragut's Naval victory in Mobile Harbor. The *Hartford* engaging the Confederate Ram *Tennessee*.

Updated engraving of the City of Mobile Museum.

Tennessee had only undergone the shot and shell from the wooden vessels and found herself impervious to them. Now she was to undergo the severest test of her short battle career. Her officers saw with horror that the *Manhattan,* sister ship of the sunken *Tecumseh,* was preparing to run out her 15-inch gun. It was at that time the largest naval gun in the world. Reported Lieutenant Wharton:

> The "Monongahela" was hardly clear of us when a hideous-looking monster came creeping up on our port side, whose slowly revolving turret revealed the cavernous depths of a mammoth gun. "Stand clear of the port side!" I shouted. A moment after a thunderous report shook us all while a blast of dense sulphurous smoke covered our port-holes, and 440 pounds of iron, impelled by sixty pounds of powder, admitted daylight through our side, where, before it struck us, there had been over two feet of solid wood, covered with five inches of solid iron. This was the only 15-inch shot that hit us fair. It did not come through; the inside netting caught the splinters, and there were no casualties from it. I was glad to find myself alive after that shot.[55]

If these great guns had been handled a little more effectively, the sides of the ram would soon have been breached. All the monitors were now bombarding the beleaguered ram with shot at short range. She fired her guns furiously, but her 7 inch and 6.4 inch Brooke rifles had no effect on the iron ships.

It was found that the incessant firing of the *Chickasaw* had loosened the metal on the rear of the casemate. She had fired about fifty shots at the same general area, and it was feared that the iron would fall right off the casemate. One well-placed shot from her guns jammed the iron cover of the stern port shut, and the gun

---

[55] This was the maximum charge of powder then used in the 15-inch guns. It was afterward found that they would stand one hundred pounds with a proportionate gain of the velocity and battering power of the projectile. Scharf, p. 568 (footnote).

Farragut's Victory in Mobile Bay – The capture of the Confederate ram *Tennessee*. – Sketched by Robert Weir.

Harper's Weekly, September 10, 1864

could not be run out to be fired.[56] Admiral Buchanan, who had taken personal charge of the battery, called below for some mechanics to repair it. Four men came up; two of them held the bolt back while the others struck the hinge-pin with sledge hammers. The admiral was standing close by directing the proceedings. One mechanic had braced his back upon the shield while working the pin out. At that moment an 11-inch shot from the *Chickasaw* hit the shield where the mechanic was leaning. The shot did not penetrate, but the tremendous concussion broke the mechanic into pieces. Said Captain Johnston, "... his remains had to be taken up with a shovel, placed in a bucket, and thrown overboard." The same shot caused splinters of iron to fly inside the shield, one killing a sailor and another breaking Buchanan's leg below the knee. Buchanan called for Johnston and turned command of the ship over to him.[57] Almost as if he had prophesied it in his speech before the fight, the old man was laid to one side, and all around him his own men worked their guns, not one looking to his aid. Here is the account of Admiral Buchanan's being wounded as reported by Surgeon Conrad:

> An aide came down the ladder in great haste and said, "Doctor, the admiral is wounded!" "Well, bring him below," I replied. "I can't do it," he answered; "I haven't time. I am carrying orders for Captain Johnston." So up I went; asked some officer whom I saw, "Where is the admiral?" "Don't know," he replied, "We are all at work loading and firing. Got too much to do to think of anything else." Then I looked for the gallant commander myself, and, lying curled up under the sharp angle of the roof, I discovered the white-haired old man. He was grim, silent, and uttered no sound in his great pain. I went up to him and asked, "Admiral, are you badly hurt?" "I don't know," he replied; but I saw one of his legs crushed under his body, and, as I

---

[56] Lewis, *Famous American*, p. 246.
[57] Johnson, p. 404.

could get no help, raised him up with great caution and, clasping his arms around my neck, carried him on my back down the ladder to the cock-pit, his broken leg slapping against me as I moved slowly along. . . .[58]

The men inside the *Tennessee* were now undergoing a hell, the horrors of which can only be imagined. Before ten o'clock, and sometime during the bombardment of the *Chickasaw*, the smokestack, weakened by the rammings, gave way.[59] Smoke filled the entire gundeck and the temperature rose to a terrific heat of over 120 degrees.[60] The cannonades from the enemy fleet were so numerous that the noise was one continuous roar. Orders could be passed only by shouting close to a man's ear, and the reverberations were so intense that the men's noses bled.[61] To make the scene thoroughly uncomfortable, the tremendous shock from striking shot caused the nuts and washers to strip off the bolts holding the iron on the sides and to ricochet about in the shield, severely wounding the men.[62] In all the punishment, no man flinched from his duty; the monotonous load and fire, load and fire being their only action.

Shortly before Buchanan was wounded, one of the monitors had shot away the exposed rudder chains, and the relieving tackle was brought into play; but this, too, was shot away in about an hour.[63] Buchanan had previously headed the ship in the direction of Fort Morgan in a vain attempt to bring the fort into the battle. It was in this direction that the ship was slowly moving when she lost all her steering tackle.[64] The enemy, seeing how she

---

[58] Lewis, *Admiral Franklin Buchanan,* p. 237.
[59] Scharf, p. 569.
[60] William N. Taft, *Photographic History of the Civil War* (New York: Review of Reviews Co., 1912), p. 249.
[61] Lewis, *Admiral Franklin Buchanan,* p. 235.
[62] Green and Frost, p. 228.
[63] Bonaparte, p. 582. In the battle, an 11-inch shot fell on the iron cover of the rudder chain groove, jamming the chains so they could not be moved.
[64] Scharf, p. 570.

lay, took positions around her and determined to crush her with a rain of shot and shell. The *Tennessee* had enough steam to turn her screw slowly and could fire three aimless guns at anything that came in front of them. Other than this, she was now perfectly helpless.[65] Then, for about thirty minutes, the *Tennessee* took the bombardment. In all that time, she never brought a gun to bear or did anything in retaliation.[66]

Johnston surveyed the scene and went to the cockpit where the admiral was lying on the surgeon's table. He reported to him the sad state of affairs and awaited his decision. The admiral said, "Well, Johnston, fight to the last! Then to save these brave men, when there is no longer any hope, surrender."[67] After hearing the old man's advice, Johnston returned to the gundeck. Through observation slits in the side, he saw the vessels of the opposing fleet maneuvering to ram him. He saw that the casemate at the stern was so weakened that, with a few good shots from the enemy, the iron would fall. They were surrounded by a ring of fire and could not bring a gun to bear. Then Johnston felt that to surrender was the best thing.[68]

Early in the combat, the *Tennessee*'s ensign had been shot away. Another ensign had been fastened to a gun scraper and thrust through the grating on the top of the shield. Not wanting to ask his own men to perform the task, Johnston himself stepped out of the protection of the casemate and onto the top of the shield into a hail of shot and shell. Disdaining enemy fire, he lowered the Confederate flag. Still the monitors kept up their fire; the *Ossipee,*

---

[65] Scharf, p. 570.
[66] Lewis, *Admiral Franklin Buchanan,* p. 238.
[67] Lewis, *Admiral Franklin Buchanan,* p. 238.
[68] Lewis, *Admiral Franklin Buchanan,* p. 238.

Engraving from Scarf's *History of the Confederate States Navy.*

Monongahela, Lackawanna, and *Hartford,* which had been closing in to ram, continued their courses. Johnston realized that the signal had not been seen. He then decided "with an almost bursting heart," to display the white flag; and grasping a staff and white cloth again stepped out onto that perilous position and (as he says)

> ... placed it in the same spot where but a few moments before had floated the proud flag for whose honor I would also cheerfully have sacrificed my own life if I could possibly have become the only victim.[69]

> "Suddenly," says Lieutenant Kenney, signal officer of the "Hartford", "the terrific cannonading ceased, and from every ship rang out cheer after cheer as the weary men realized that at last the ram was captured and the day won."[70]

Johnston, acting for the wounded Buchanan, surrendered the admiral's sword to Commander Leroy of the *Ossipee.* Captain Percival Drayton of the *Hartford* later said to the defeated Johnston: "You have one consolation, Johnston; no one can say that you have not nobly defended the honor of the Confederate flag today."[71]

[69] Lewis, *Admiral Franklin Buchanan,* p. 238.
[70] Green and Frost, p. 229.
[71] Johnson, p. 405.

So ended the naval encounter of August 5, 1864. Combined Federal land and naval operations would defeat the defenses of Mobile by April 12, 1865. No new tactical maneuvers were added to naval annals by this struggle; it hastened, perhaps, the collapse of the Confederacy. But the Battle of Mobile Bay entered popular history. This happened on the strength of two powerful icons. First, the image of the hero lashed to the rigging of his embattled ship, which is as old as Odysseus and the Sirens. Second, a cry: "Damn the torpedoes, full speed ahead!" Though it is unlikely that Farragut spoke them in battle, what other words better suit a rallying cry for our nation?

Buchanan, only faintly recalled, is trapped inside history books and museums. Yet he, too, has his place in the national myth as invincible loser, the lone rebel who doggedly takes on overwhelming odds, foregoing the protection of his "fort," where security would only prolong defeat.

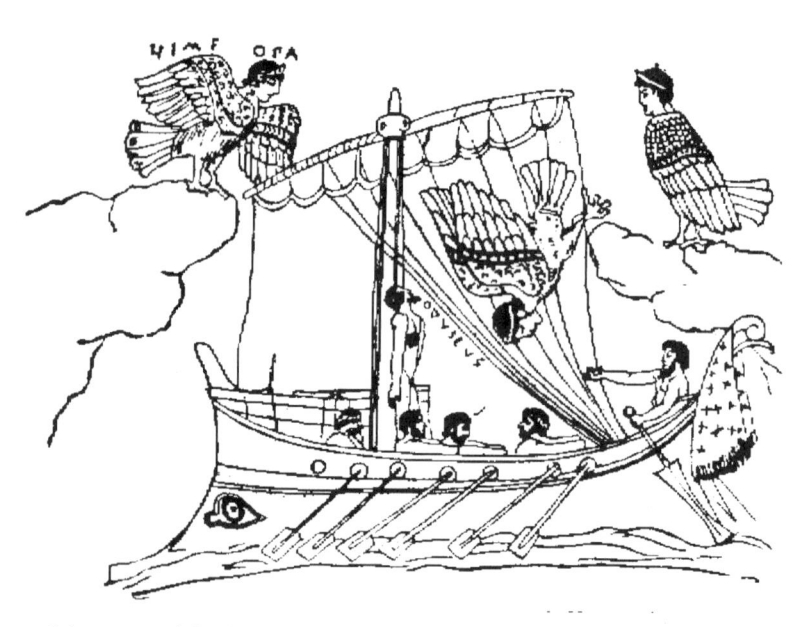

Odysseus and the Sirens is used with the permission of the British Museum.

APPENDIX

1. A list of casualties in the Federal fleet:

	Hits	Killed	Wounded	Prisoners
Hartford	20	25	28	0
Brooklyn	30	11	43	0
Lackawanna	5	4	35	0
Oneida	15	8	30	0
Monongahela	5	0	6	0
Metacomet	10	1	2	0
Ossipee	4	1	2	0
Richmond	5	0	2	0
Galena	9	0	1	0
Octorara	11	1	10	0
Kennebec	2	1	6	0
Tecumseh	—	114	0	4
Manhattan	9	0	0	0
Winnebago	19	0	0	0
Chickasaw	5	0	0	0
Totals	149	166	170	4

Actual battle casualties, excepting the men who drowned in the *Tecumseh*, were 52 killed and 170 wounded.

2. A list of casualties in the Confederate fleet:

	Killed	Wounded	Prisoners
Tennessee	2	8	198
Gaines	2	3	0
Selma	8	7	ent. crew
Morgan	0	1	0

Entire Confederate casualties were 12 killed and 19 wounded.

3. Official Confederate reports never acknowledged that the *Tecumseh* was struck by a torpedo. Many officers were of the opinion that she was struck by a shot from Fort Morgan. To present this side of the question, this letter is inserted:

Mobile, Ala., Oct. 4, 1864

Dear General: I have the honor respectfully to state that I was on duty at Fort Morgan when the enemy's fleet entered the bay on the morning of August 5, ultimo, and saw the monitor "Tecumseh" when she went down. I am of the opinion that she sunk before reaching the line of torpedoes. This opinion is entertained by such other of the officers of the fort as witnessed the sinking and by the pilots on lookout duty and privates who had been detailed to assist in planting the torpedoes. I saw distinctly the bottom of the "Tecumseh" and could discover no damage to show it was struck by a torpedo. She was sunk about 500 or 600 yards from the fort. . . . No ship of the enemy, wooden or iron passed through the gap, however, (the gap between fort and buoy) nor according to my judgement within 300 yards of it . . . . I have been stationed at the fort for over three years, and claim to be perfectly familiar with the distance of all objects within sight—such as stakes, buoys, etc.

Very respectively, your obedient servant
J. W. Whiting,
Captain, First Alabama Battalion, Artillery

Major-General D. H. Maury.

BIBLIOGRAPHY

Abbot, Willis J. *The Naval History of the United States*. New York: Dodd Mead and Company, 1896.

Andrews, C. C. *History of the Campaign of Mobile*. New York: D. Van Nostrand, 1867.

Delaney, Caldwell. *Confederate Mobile*. Mobile: The Haunted Book Shop, 1971.

Frothingham, J. P. *Sea Fighters from Drake to Farragut*. New York: Scribner's Sons, 1927.

Green, F. and Frost, H. *Some Famous Sea Fights*. New York and London: The Century Co., 1927.

Hill, Jim Dan. *Sea Dogs of the Sixties*. Minneapolis: The University of Minnesota Press, 1935.

Johnson, Robert Underwood. *The Battles and Leaders of the Civil War*. New York: The Century Co., 1887.

Lewis, Charles Lee. *Admiral Franklin Buchanan*. Baltimore: The Norman Remington Co., 1929.

―――. *Famous American Naval Officers*. Boston: L. C. Page and Company, 1924.

Official Records of the Union and Confederate Navies in the War of the Rebellion. Published under direction of C. J. Bonaparte. Series I, vol. 21. Published by Charles W. Stewart. Washington Government Printing Office, 1906.

Poore, Ralph. "Yankee Farragut Born and Reared in Dixie." *Mobile Press Register*, Sunday, August 5, 1979.

Scharf, J. T. *History of the Confederate States Navy*. New York: Rogers and Sherwood, 1887.

Shippen, Edward. *Naval Battles of America*. Philadelphia: P. W. Ziegler Co., 1905.

Taft, William H. *Photographic History of the Civil War*. New York: Review of Reviews Co., 1912.

Thorpe, F. N. *History of North America*. Philadelphia: George Barrie's Sons, 1906.

West, Richard S. *Gideon Wells, Lincoln's Navy Dept*. Indianapolis: Bobbs-Merrill Co., 1943.

Franklin Buchanan on the *Tennessee*

Some of the dialogue in this portrait of Admiral Franklin Buchanan is quoted from the memoirs of Fleet Surgeon Daniel B. Conrad as contained in C. L. Lewis's Admiral Franklin Buchanan *(Baltimore: The Norman Remington Company, 1929). J. T. Scharf's* History of the Confederate States Navy *(New York: Rogers and Sherwood, 1887) also contains recollections of words spoken during the battle and provided insight into the characters portrayed. The greater part of the dialogue is, however, imaginary, the work of an author indebted to those participants in the Battle of Mobile Bay who struggled to shape the terrible things they had endured by putting words to paper.*

THE SUN HAD JUST SET. A GENTLE SWELL WAS COMING INTO THE BAY from the Gulf. A small boat moved across the waters. Though it was still light, the oarblades made the water twinkle with phosphorescence. An old man sat with crossed legs in the stern seat watching the pools of light slip by the sides of the boat.

The boat went on in silence. Overhead, terns and pelicans were flying out into the Gulf to roost on the sand islands. The old man looked in that direction. He was looking for tiny twinkling lights on the water, lights he knew were there but could not see.

The rowboat was pulling toward an ironclad lying about a mile off Mobile Point. The old man was watching the ironclad now and he was thinking about delays. There were delays in Selma, as the ship lay with her naked ribs pointing to the sky. He thought of supply delays in Mobile; it took time to buy even a few sacks of yams.

The delay on Dog River was the worst. He remembered the poor ship stuck helplessly on the Dog River bar. So unladylike, he remembered. Then they brought the caissons down and sank them and strapped them to her sides. Then the pumps broke and the

A portrait of Admiral Franklin Buchanan. Photograph courtesy of Caldwell Delaney, Director, Musuem of Mobile.

divers cursed, but, finally, she wrenched herself loose from the mud so they could take the ugly caissons off her sides.

> Delay has done it. My ship will never taste the waters of the Gulf. The iron on these ships presses them too deep. *Virginia's* draft—22 feet—keel sliding in the mud at Hampton Roads. The difficulties of movement through shoal water to attack the *Congress* were formidable, but I did it—fired at my own brother, too. He was on the *Congress*. Yes. Then they hit my leg. Then the *Monitor* came.

The boat had reached the side of the ironclad now. The sailors got out and respectfully held the little boat close to her side. The old man slowly stood up in the stern. He was crippled, but no one dared to help him. He grasped a stanchion and lifted himself out onto the deck.

The captain stepped forward. "Welcome back, Admiral. I trust you have news from Fort Morgan."

"You are correct, sir. Where's Conrad? I have drugs for him and news for us all. We'll go to the cockpit."

Four men sat at a little chart table. Dr. Conrad was smoking a pipe and blew the smoke toward an ornate oil lamp hanging overhead. The heat from the chimney pulled the smoke toward the ceiling. The air in the cockpit was still and stiflingly hot.

"Gentlemen. I shall be brief, for I am tired. I've just left General Page's rooms at the fort. Granger landed a considerable force on Dauphin Island yesterday—about the mid-point of the island. He is making deliberate progress toward Fort Gaines. General Page and I expect Farragut will attempt an entry on high tide."

There was little to say. Lieutenant Wharton was thinking of his Brooke rifled cannon and how many of his primers would be defective tomorrow. Captain Johnston was thinking about speed and boilers. He was wondering how far one tempted the rackety boilers of the *Tennessee* to force it over six knots an hour. Fleet Surgeon Conrad was thinking of how far his laudanum would go if he had amputations on shipboard. But Admiral Buchanan was thinking of delay again and failure.

Perhaps if the tide had been right at Dog River, there would have been time. David Farragut would have been surprised and perhaps Fort Pickens would have been recaptured according to plan. I would be in the Gulf—out there my leg wouldn't pain me so and I wouldn't feel as old as I do. It was bad for the men to see me almost crawl out of the gig tonight.

After some time the admiral spoke again. "We must sleep as much as possible tonight. Tomorrow may be a difficult day for us all. Gentlemen, goodnight."

Lieutenant Wharton and Captain Johnston left the cabin while Dr. Conrad and Admiral Buchanan stepped out onto a spot upon the iron back of the ship called "The admiral's deck." Sleeping on the deck was necessary in the heat of August.

The admiral removed his cap for the first time. A large ruff of white hair circled the back of his head, a contrast to his thin face. Seeing his cot Buchanan said irritably, "Dr. Conrad, you needn't have arranged my mosquito bar. I'm old, but still perfectly capable!"

The doctor nervously twisted his fat little hands together as he replied. "I thought, sir, that you would be tired after your interview at the fort. It was no bother to me at all, I assure you."

"Excuse my tongue, Conrad. I am tired. I'm a little tired of the whole affair and I'm tired of the battle tomorrow already. It's to be defensive, of course. It needn't have been but for—for many things that don't matter now. Goodnight."

Dr. Conrad did not choose to speak again, so the hot night was passed in perfect quiet.

A fog had arisen about three that morning, but, as its vestiges were brushed from the face of the waters, there was seen far out in the Gulf a black smudge of smoke from the four monitors and fourteen screw steamers of David Farragut's fleet. At 5:45 the procession began. The monitors took the lead and the wooden ships followed, "balanced to partners," lashed fast side by side. After six o'clock the *Tennessee*'s old quartermaster, his voice gruff with importance, awakened Admiral Franklin Buchanan.

"Admiral, the officer of the deck bids me report that the enemy's fleet is under way."

The admiral rolled from his bed. The squat black monitors had begun their progress from anchorages inside of Sand Island Light. At 6:47 a puff of smoke and flame issued from the turret of the lead *Tecumseh* and a 440-pound bolt splashed into the water off Fort Morgan.

"Is Captain Johnston in the pilot house?"

"Yes sir."

The old man hurried to a speaking tube. "Captain Johnston, head for the leading vessel of the enemy and fight each one as they pass."

The *Tennessee* began to move to face the enemy. Alabama coal was thrown into boilers from the rolling mills of Atlanta. The piston rod began its first, slow seven-foot stroke and the screw made its first slow turn. Rudder chains clanked across the open deck, the gun crews loaded the Brooke rifles, and the iron prow began to turn toward the leading vessel.

The admiral arrived in the pilot house stuffing in his blouse and adjusting his cap, tugging straight his admiral's jacket. "Captain, that's T.A.M. Craven in the *Tecumseh*. He's out to get us today."

The captain peered through a little observation slit, "I'd love to put a shot through that ugly cheese box."

Buchanan smiled now for the first time, a smile exercising long dormant muscles. He was pacing the pilot house and barely limping, "They say she has ten inches of iron on her turret, Captain. Would you say it's as good as six of Selma's best? We're going to find out."

The two ships moved slowly toward one another. Firing was general in all quarters now except for these two silent ironclads. They were reserving their first fire for one another. The admiral was peering tensely through the observation slit and on the *Tecumseh*. T. A. M. Craven was watching the *Tennessee* from his squat conning tower atop the turret.

"Orderly, relay a message to Lieutenant Wharton not to fire until we are in actual contact. Johnston, move to the west and behind the line of torpedoes."

"But, sir, she's not going to cross that line to us!"

"I told you I know Craven. He's out to get us today and he's out for an admiralty too. I'll caution you to watch the black buoy."

To the west of the black buoy were 180 mines in a triple row, stretching in a line across the mouth of the Bay. The monitor turned toward the *Tennessee*'s new position and crept toward the western side of the buoy. The *Tecumseh* was a hundred yards from the *Tennessee* when a fountain of water spurted up by its side. It jerked and heeled over. Its slowly revolving screw was the last to go under. It sank in thirty seconds.

"Don't fire on the ship picking up survivors, head for the *Hartford*." Buchanan was pacing from slit to slit while Farragut's flagship loomed larger and larger in his vision.

"Swing hard to port, attempt to ram!"

"She'll outdistance us before we reach her!"

"For God's sake, try, Captain!"

It was useless. The swifter flagship evaded the clumsy thrust. Buchanan had to content himself with meeting the rest of the fleet as it passed by. Almost every ship got a remembrance from him; the *Hartford*'s escape had whetted his anger.

At 8:40 Fort Morgan ceased fire. The fleet had successfully passed the range of her guns. Admiral Buchanan had kept the *Tennessee* under the fort's guns, so the Federal fleet was now far from him. The *Tennessee* moved to the northeast of Fort Morgan while her cooks began serving a delayed breakfast of salt pork and hard tack.

"I don't want any breakfast, thank you, Doctor. Please leave me. I am trying to think."

The fleet surgeon was most happy to leave him and returned immediately to the pilot house to finish his own breakfast.

The admiral was thinking of his childhood in Baltimore. When he and his brother were little, they used to ride down pine trees.

> You inched to the top, never leaning to the side; then kicked out into space, falling in a curve. But it took a lot of scrubbing to get the rosin off afterwards.

Hampton Roads flashed across his mind again. His wound robbed him of command when the first two ironclads turned on each other.

> Worden and Catesby Jones were like children with Christmas toys. Oh to have been in command! The *Monitor's* gunners chalked my ship's position on the gun deck because the spinning turret dizzied them so. Then they rubbed the chalk up with their feet. Four years at it. The night Tatnall set the torch to my *Virginia*. The magazines went up, one, two, three, and she was left on the bank to rot. Will I be?

The Federal fleet was now anchored far up the Bay. The sheeted dead were laid along the scuppers waiting to be buried. The Federals looked down the Bay to the *Tennessee*. "We'll eat and then go down the Bay to finish her," they said.

And Buchanan was still pacing up and down the high top deck of his iron ship, but he had put his past behind him. He had finished remembering the pine trees, and Hampton Roads, and the *Virginia's* burning. Once he knew what he must do, he left off remembering.

The staff had finished breakfast and were now standing on the top deck watching the admiral. No one spoke; the uneven sound of the limping pace seemed quite loud. At the end of one of his pacings, Buchanan stopped in front of the captain, "Follow them up, Johnston. We can't let them off that way."

Little waves slapped over the sunken prow as the iron ship turned to the north. The crew on the deck outside the shield looked with amazement toward the top deck. The admiral was attacking seventeen warships—alone.

Dr. Conrad attempted to engage him in conversation.

"Are you really going into the fleet, sir?"

"I am, sir."

The surgeon whispered to a nearby officer, "Well, we'll never come out of there whole."

The admiral heard this remark and turned upon the embarrassed doctor, his face as hard as the sides of his ship.

"That's my lookout, sir!"

The Federals came to meet Buchanan halfway. The wooden ships led, for they were the fastest, and formed a circle around the *Tennessee*. The larger ships were ramming while the rest pelted her iron sides with solid shot. Then the monitors arrived. The *Tecumseh*'s sister, the *Manhattan*, ran out her pug-nosed 15-inch gun and breached the *Tennessee*'s side with a 440-pound flat head bolt. After this shot the admiral descended to the gundeck and directed the firing himself. There was no more maneuvering to be done. The monitor *Chickasaw* had carried away the rudder chains with a lucky shot, and with the loss of the smokestack, the boilers ceased to draw.

Lieutenant Wharton found the admiral near the bow and began shouting in his ear, over the uproar, "The stern port shutter is jammed. We can't run out the gun!"

"Take charge here, Wharton, and I'll unstick it myself."

Buchanan threaded his way down the littered gundeck. His men were loading and firing monotonously, some stripped to the waist, blood streaming from their noses down their chests. The concussion inside the shield was terrific. The cannonades had fused into one continuous roar. Nuts and washers, stripped from their bolts by shot hitting the side, were ricocheting about the walls.

"I want four men here to fix this shutter; relay that order, please."

"Yes, sir."

Some firemen came from below with sledges and hammers. They all set to work with Buchanan stooping beside them shouting instructions in their ears. One of the men had braced his back against the wall of the shield. Outside, the turret of the monitor *Chickasaw* trundled around on its track, exposing her 11-inch gun. She fired and the steel shot struck directly outside the port shutter of the *Tennessee*. The shot did not enter the shield but a flurry of steel splinters sprayed through the half-open port. Buchanan slumped across the barrel of the inactive Brooke rifle. The fireman braced against the wall was only a broken pile of flesh at the admiral's feet.

The old man was conscious and managed to drag himself across the bloody deck to the edge of the shield before he collapsed. His good leg was twisted under him in a grotesque bend. There was a stream of blood running down the gold stripe on his trousers' leg. The admiral caught the foot of a powder boy running by and pulled him down close to him, "Get Captain Johnston here at once, hurry now!"

Johnston quickly arrived and knelt at the admiral's head. Buchanan said to him, "Well, Johnston, they've got me. You'll have to look out for her now. This is your fight, you know."

Johnston knelt silently by the admiral's head; he was near tears and was yearning to pay some personal attention to his leader's physical condition. Instead, he stood and saluted. "All right, sir, I'll do the best I know how."

From his position under the angle of the sloping shield, Buchanan could see the moving feet of the port gun crew. He felt drowsy. Sometimes he thought he was in the *Virginia* again.

> The smoke, noise, heat, concussion, bleeding noses—it's all the same. Other things are the same too. The insufficiency of materials, the defective engines, exposed rudder chains—the same; poor goods, uncomplaining, ill-trained crew—the same. Hampton Roads, testing our new playthings with fire while the two nations waited. No, I'm in Mobile Bay. David Farragut has broken my good leg and my ship is dying. There's not fifty pounds in the boilers.

He twisted his body until it faced the shield, put his arm upon his face, and clenched his teeth.

Dr. Conrad was tapping him on the back, "Admiral, are you badly hurt?"

"I don't know."

"We'll soon see; put your arms around my neck when I get down by you. I'm taking you to the cockpit."

The doctor set off down the gundeck, stooping under the weight of the admiral. His own trouser' leg reddened as the broken leg slapped gently against it.

The admiral lay without moving on the surgeon's table as Conrad hovered over his leg. He did not turn his head as Captain Johnston entered the cockpit. Before the captain could finish a report on the state of the ship, he was quietly interrupted, "Well Johnston, fight to the last. Then to save these brave men, when there is no longer any hope, surrender. I'm sorry you must surrender her for me."

Johnston left the cockpit and some few minutes later the bombardment ceased. Buchanan could hear the sound of cheering come faintly through the walls of pine and iron. He was racked with a chill and trembled from head to foot. He was pulling a blanket about his body when a very young Federal officer burst into the cockpit.

"Admiral Farragut sends his solicitations. He has learned that you were wounded and, on the strength of your past friendship with him, begs you to be moved to the *Hartford* and be sent to Pensacola tonight for the best medical treatment."

The officer finished his speech and stood awkwardly staring about the dingy cockpit.

Franklin Buchanan sat up on the surgeon's table and clenched his fists. His hair was matted with dark blood. He spoke with absolute firmness, "I cannot pretend friendship with Admiral Farragut and request that I be given that same treatment received by the rest of my men."

* * *

The seams of his ship were started. Water rose in the bilge at six inches per hour. The boiler fires were dying. Cooling nitrous smoke was sinking to the lower levels of the shield. The *Tennessee* became Federal property, lay at dock never to fight again, and was auctioned for scrap in New Orleans on November 17, 1867.

Farragut sent a communique to Brigadier General R.L. Page, commander of Fort Morgan, informing him that Admiral Buchanan had lost his leg. He proposed that the *Metacomet*, carrying Buchanan and the Confederate and Federal wounded, be allowed to pass under the guns of Fort Morgan to federally held Pensacola for medical treatment. The *Metacomet* was to return without the addition of any military goods. Page acceded to this generous offer. Buchanan, however, did not lose the leg. He left sailoring on his two feet.

The Admiral wrote a dry report of the battle to Confederate Naval Secretary Mallory. The report confirms that he did not consider it remarkable to have attacked alone the largest naval fleet then assembled.

Buchanan attempted to resume life in Maryland. He had entered the United States Navy at age fifteen and later achieved the distinction of becoming first superintendent of the Annapolis Naval Academy, 1845-47. He had led sailors onto Japanese soil under Mathew Perry. Thinking Maryland was to secede, he resigned his naval commission. When his native state did not leave the Union, he reapplied and was refused. He did not waver, but set about creating the Confederate States Navy. After 1864 the Admiral lived out his life on land. Offered the presidency of the Maryland Agricultural College, he served but one year, 1868-1869. Returning to Alabama, he served as State Manager for The Life Association of America 1870-1871. He lasted eighteen months in that position. Living longer than he might have imagined possible during those miasmal summer days on Mobile Bay, he died May, 1874 at his home, "The Rest", in Talbot County, Maryland.